# Blackfeet Raiders

## Nomads of the North

**Robert D. Bolen, B.A.**

3

Dedication Page

I dedicate this work to my wife, Doris Anne

# ILLUSTRATIONS

5

# CONTENTS

# Blackfeet Raiders

## Nomads of the North

# Acknowledgements

My deepest thanks to Teresa, owner of Azusa Publishing, L.L.C. for all of the Indian post cards that she has graciously allowed me to use in this text. The pictures make the book in my estimation. Her website and ad for authentic Indian postcards is in the back of the book. I recommend that you try her web site.

I would like to express my gratitude to Renate Reiss for the use of the ten wonderful prints of paintings by the marvelous artist, Winold Reiss. Thank you so much for the use of the print, "Nobody Has Pity on Me," to Sally King, Art Curator and to the Burlington Northern Santa Fe Railway. I would like to thank the Smithsonian Institute for the Chief Washakie village photograph and also the Library of Congress for the excellent ancient wickiup photo.

I would also like to thank my friend, Rosemary Devinney for answering my questions about the Shoshone people, every time I call her. Rosemary is the Curator of the Fort Hall Shoshone-Bannock Museum.

Thanks also to Shirley Crowfoot of the Alberta Piegan Blackfoot Nation for the question and answer period about her people. It helped me quite a bit in my writing; it is an honor.

Thank you to Len Sodenkamp for his unique artist's rendition of "Buffalo Hunter on Horseback."

I would like to thank the Wal-Mart Photo staff for their processing of pictures and to Fed-ex Office for their help in preparation. Last, but not least, my sincerest thanks to Lightning Source for their fine job of printing this publication.

Kudos to Susan Raney, for the beautiful job that she did, editing the manuscript. I could not have done it without her, thank you Susan.

#3. Beautiful Blackfeet Princess
(Photograph Courtesy of Azusa Publishing, LLC)

# Foreword

Nearly 15,000 years ago, after the last Ice Age, prehistoric man crossed over the Bering Straits to the Americas. Early man moved in waves onto the American Continent. They journeyed far bringing their families. Women carried their young in cradleboards on their shoulders. When early man first entered the continent, large game animals existed: the woolly mammoth, mastodon, giant tree sloth, bison-bison and saber-toothed tiger were killed at a distance using an ancient spear thrower, called the atlatl; a spear could be launched 100 yards with a hand-held spear chucker.

The theory that the largest animals were first to face extinction has long been proven. The mammoth, mastodon elephants and other large species were first to die off. As the size of the largest animals diminished, the size of the projectile point did, too. After the atlatl, 2,000 years ago, the bow and arrow was adopted and the utilization of the atlatl slowed.

Paleontologists theorize from the size of the skulls found that the first horses most likely were zebras. The "Hagerman Horse" in Idaho is such an example. One theory is that wild horses were hunted by the Indians and eaten, opposed to being ridden, and became extinct in America. Many tribes scattered over the land, which teemed in fauna and flora. It was a new world. In their ancestral ways, these tribes migrated following massive herds of caribou and bison. The nomads dwelled in tents of animal skins. They spoke different languages and represented various peoples. Aboriginal people in mass quantities entered the Americas. Many tribes established boundaries and remained sedentary, only moving around locally in season, but the Blackfoot Indians were nomads, always on the move.

Animals made a major difference in the lives of the Plains Indians. These were the buffalo, deer, eagle, horse and the mountain lion. Animals were sacred to them. The buffalo provided meat to live. The hide made robes, worn fur side out that kept them warm in winter, as well as moccasins. The buffalo hides covered their teepees. From bones, hooves and horns they crafted utilities. Deerskin made clothing, like war shirts. Eagle feathers made beautiful war bonnets. The horse totally changed their movements and war. The mountain lion skins were revered and used for coverings.

The large confederation of the Blackfoot Nation claim to be the oldest indigenous people on the western Plains. It is theorized they had been in place for over 6,000 years in Canada. Some migrated into America, across the Rocky Mountain Range, circa 3,000 B.C. and became Horse Indians of the Northwestern Plains. The Blackfeet, living in Montana, were semi-nomadic and constantly raided the villages of the Shoshoni, Bannock, Flathead, Nez Perce and other tribes for horses in the region now known as Idaho. They roamed free on the northwestern plains less than 150 years ago.

#4. Wickiup Aboriginal Dwelling
Courtesy of the Library of Congress

# Chapter One
## First Nation

Aboriginal peoples came from the northwest to lodge in a land that would be known as Alberta, in North America. It is estimated that they came as early as 6,000 B.P. These were the ancestors of the Blackfoot tribe as we now know it. Extended bands of Blackfoot peoples dwelled there. The bands grew into a league of four Blackfoot tribes: the Blood (*Kainai*), *Piegan (Pekuni), Siksika (Sakitapix)* and the "Small Robes," the southernmost tribe in Canada. The Blackfoot people were members of the wide spread Algonquian language stock, ranging from Canada to the Great Lakes and the Atlantic. All four tribes of the Blackfoot Nation spoke the same language. *Apikunipuyi*, in their tongue, meant speakers of the same language. The four tribes were united as one nation, language and religion. Allies were the Sarcee Indians.

Their speech made a linguistic shift, becoming the old (Proto-Algonquian) and the new Blackfoot dialects. The Blackfoot language branched off from the Algonquian stock first; an indicator that they were here first and that Proto-Algonquian had originated circa 3,000 years B.P. with the Blackfeet in Montana. The Blackfoot in the Alberta area date back to circa 6,000 B.P. at Heads-Smashed-In Buffalo Jump. The Algonquian dialect of the Blackfoot tribe differed drastically from that spoken by speakers of the same stock dwelling in the Great Lakes region. Linguists say that the Blackfoot dialect was the first dialect to evolve, indicating that they were the first to enter the continent. The four Blackfoot tribes' dialects varied some.

One theory of archeologists to explain the separation of language speakers is that a large band of natives may have crossed the Bering Straits and then split; one group continued southward, while the other band swung toward the southeast into middle America. Another theory is that the Blackfoot first settled in the Great Lakes region, then drifted back west into Canada and Montana. They believe that they were always in one location.

The Algonquian speakers formerly occupied more area than any other language stock, reaching from Newfoundland to the Rocky Mountains and from Pamlico Sound in North Carolina to the Churchill River in Canada. Twenty-seven Algonquian tribes stretched across the American continent from the Rockies to the Atlantic.

#5. Arapaho Chief, Algonquian Speaker
(Photograph Courtesy of Azusa Publishing, LLC)

14

The Northern Piegan (*Aapa'tohsipika'ni*) of the *Niitsi'tapi, the* (Blackfoot Confederacy) are known as the *Piikani* or Pekuni tribe. Piegan bands averaged 10 to 30 lodges, the equivalent of 80 to 240 people. They were considered the strongest tribe in the confederation.

The *Siksika* are the Blackfoot tribe. Siksika, in their tongue, literally means "Black footed," or "Blackfoot." Another word for Blackfoot in their native tongue was *Nitsitapii*. They were the northernmost tribe in what is now Canada. This band became the Blackfoot tribe. Legend has it that they were called Blackfoot because their moccasin soles were blackened from walking across the ashes of the burned prairie. Another premise is that they actually dyed their moccasins black, but their moccasins were black.

Other Blackfoot peoples of the Blackfoot Nation moved on into America. The Blackfoot people were some of the earliest tribes to arrive on the High Plains. They chose a land on the Northern Plains, nestled in the Rocky Mountains to inhabit. The southern Piegan Indians in America were called the "*Ahpikuni*," in the Blackfoot tongue. In America, they spell the tribal name, Blackfeet. I asked a Blackfeet maiden why the name was Blackfeet and not Blackfoot. Her reply was, "Well, we have two feet." In Canada it is spelled Blackfoot.

There is a Blackfoot Indian legend about a young brave who wanted to view the buffalo plunge over a cliff from the valley below. Instead, his mangled body was found underneath the buffalo carcasses, with his head smashed in. He was forever remembered and they named the site, Head-Smashed-in-Buffalo Jump, Canada (*Estipah-Skikikinikots* in the Blackfoot language). This jump was a favorite of the Blackfoot. This buffalo jump has existed in the foothills of the Rocky Mountains for nearly 6,000 years.

The Native Blackfoot people stampeded buffalo that were grazing on Porcupine Hill. The buffalo jump took advantage of a bison herd grazing adjacent to the cliff. Lanes were built, leading to the edge of the cliff. The shaman would either start a fire or wave a blanket, giving war-whoops in order to drive the buffalo along the stone drive lanes, 300 meters to the cliff's edge, and plummeted over the cliff 10 meters to their deaths.

The fall broke their legs or killed them. If the buffalo only broke their legs, their heads were smashed in by Blackfoot war clubs. Butchering stations were established below for processing. Normally, the men skinned and butchered the bison, while the women scraped and tanned the hides. The jump was abandoned by 1900, after the European conflict. Bones below the jump accumulated there for 6,000 years, 10 meters deep.

There was a Blackfoot chief named Piegan (pheasant), who led the Piegan tribe in the split from the Blackfoot tribe, called the *Pekuni* (Spotted Robes). The prehistoric Blackfoot lodged in an area that ranged from the North Saskatchewan River, in Alberta, and by the Yellowstone River on the south and the west by the headwaters of the Missouri River and 105 degrees longitude to the base of the Rocky Mountains and on the east by the Sand Hills in Saskatchewan.

The Blackfoot were in control of a huge territory. The nomadic hunters followed the bison herds from uncharted Alberta, Idaho and Montana, into Yellowstone. The tigerish Blackfoot held their ground and lodged there for hundreds of years.

After the Sun Dance, the Blackfoot festival to worship the sun, the bands divided to pursue the buffalo. They organized communal hunts. Other bands might join them there to hunt the bison. In the autumn, the bands moved to the location of their communal buffalo jump to hunt the buffalo before moving to their wintering grounds. The Piegan wintered along the Belly, Highland and Battle Rivers, for northern dwellers.

In 1670, King Charles II granted a charter to the Governor and Company of Adventurers, the right to trap for furs in Canada and unexplored lands. The Hudson's Bay Company began trading with the Indians around Hudson's Bay. In the next century, the employees of Hudson's Bay Company were trading for furs with the Assiniboine and Cree Indians on the Canadian Plain. Trader Henry Kelsey was told about the strong Blackfoot Indians that dwelled to the west.

In the 1700's, white fur traders first moved into what is now Canada, they built fur forts for the purpose of trade with the Indians. The Blackfoot were suspicious of them and did not trust them. The Assiniboine and Cree tribes, however, traded at the forts and garnered firearms, steel traps, arrowheads, knives and hatchets. The Blackfoot were excluded. The only way they could get the steel goods was through trade with other Indian tribes, capturing them from dead rivals or ambushing a party of trappers and finally traded with David Thompson of the Hudson's Bay Company.

In 1730, the Shoshonis first attacked the Blackfoot on horseback, defeating them. They attained horses shortly after the Shoshonis. The Assiniboine and Cree Indians garnered firearms early from the Hudson's Bay Company and the Piegan began to acquire rifles in trade from them. The Assiniboine, Blackfoot and Cree formed an alliance against the Shoshonis and attacked a large Shoshoni war party and began firing.

#6. "Lazy Boy" Blackfoot War Chief (Photograph Courtesy of Azusa
Publishing, LLC)

With the advantage of fire power, the siege ended in the din of blue, acrid smelling smoke, and 50 Shoshoni Indians lay dead. The Blackfoot scalped them and captured their weapons and clothes, counting coup. Most of the Shoshoni Indians broke and ran.

In 1748, the French fur traders had established forts on the lower Saskatchewan for the fur trade in Blackfoot country, the Indians called them, "Old man people." At the Treaty of Paris In 1763, the French relinquished all claim to their possessions in Canada. The French pulled out, opening up competition for trade along the Saskatchewan River.

The Northwest Company out of Montreal was formed in 1779. By 1784, they were operating in Blackfoot country. In the winter of 1787, David Thompson of the Hudson's Bay Company, wintered and traded with the Piegan Tribe on the Bow River. In 1799, the Nor Westers built "Rocky Mountain House," and began to gain a good share of the fur trade with the Piegan Indians. Rival companies built their forts in close proximity for safety's sake and were stockade posts defended by canons.

In 1781, the Piegan sent scouts ahead before attacking a Shoshoni encampment at daybreak on the Red Deer River. They found a village of dead and dying Shoshoni Indians, infected with smallpox. The Shoshonis that survived vacated the Bow River region, leaving it for the Piegan. The Piegan carried the deadly smallpox back to their lodges, infecting the village. The deadly smallpox spread and the people lay sick and dying. The Piegan made sacrifices to the evil spirit. Smallpox cut their numbers in half.

In 1787, 250 Blackfoot warriors went on the war path in western Canada, 300 miles north of the medicine line (the Canadian border). They rode 1,500 miles south and did not discover any Shoshoni Indians, but did happen upon a party of Spaniards with horses and mules. The war party attacked, giving out war-cries and the Spaniards fled, leaving the animals. The Indians scattered the Spaniards, taking the horses and mules. They did not understand that the shiny silver stones that fell on the ground were thousands of dollars worth of silver. Little did they know, nor did they care. Their prize was 30 horses, 12 mules, fine saddles and bridles.

It was estimated in 1809, that there were only 650 Blood, Northern Blackfoot and Piegan lodges all told, 1,420 warriors, and 5,200 Blackfoot people left north of the medicine line. Smallpox had taken its toll on the Blackfoot. In 1809, a North West Company post, Fort Vermillion, on the Saskatchewan River, housed 35 French Canadian employees, as well as Indian wives and children, totaling 130 people. The Indians called the

***tfl.*** Sentry on Outlook
(Photograph Courtesy of Azusa Publishing, LLC)

19

fort, "Old Man Person's lodge." When the Piegan arrived at the post, there was much pomp and celebration. Flags were flown and firearms discharged in the air. The Indians were disarmed and greeted. They sat on the floor in order of rank. Rum was served and the pipes filled with tobacco, lit and smoked.

In 1819, whooping cough killed off one-third of the Blackfeet people. In 1837, smallpox struck again, killing two-thirds of the Blackfoot Confederacy. Another smallpox plague inundated the Blackfeet Indians in 1845 and again in the winter of 1857-58.

The Piegan women erected teepees near the fort and everyone sampled the rum. It was the next day that the Piegan brought their goods to the fort and began the trade. They were poor beaver hunters; instead, they traded fox and wolf pelts that they snared.

The Indians brought fresh buffalo meat, jerky and pemmican to Fort Vermillion. The Piegan traded horses to them; a horse brought one keg of rum, a fleshing knife, a gun worm, a P.C. glass, and a flint. Favorite items of trade for the Blackfoot Indians were liquor, rifles, ammunition and tobacco. The Blackfoot had firearms early and used them to dominate surrounding tribes and gave them an advantage in war.

Guns were supplied to the Blackfoot by the Hudson's Bay Company and the North West Company. With firearms, they drove the Shoshoni, Flathead and Kutenai Indians from the Plains. The bow and arrow was no match for the trade gun, which traded for 14 beaver pelts or the equivalent at Fort George. Twenty rounds of shot cost one beaver skin; powder cost extra.

The Blackfoot traded for metal arrowheads, knives, hatchets, kettles flint and steel. Finger rings, glass beads, pigment for teepees, clothing and face paint were sold.

Tobacco came in two forms: sausage shaped (tied at the ends, marked to be cut and sold). Tobacco also came in large coils (one inch in diameter). Trade tobacco soon replaced kinnickinnick.

A large keg of whiskey traded for 30 beaver pelts at Fort George. The traders at the whiskey forts watered down the liquor before trade with the Indians, who were not accustomed to alcohol. A large keg held nine gallons (four or five quarts of high wine were topped off with water). The Blackfoot Indians called liquor "white man's water."

Around 1854, the Blackfoot raided tribes on both sides of the medicine line. They made night raids to take horses from their enemies.

#8. Sarcee Allies
(Photograph Courtesy of Azusa Publishing, LLC)

This way, they built their herds up in numbers. Coup was counted as one horse. Horses meant wealth. They attacked the Cree on the Saskatchewan River and attacked the Crow on the Yellowstone River. Blackfoot raided the Assiniboine at the mouth of the Milk River.

Guns gained in trade gave the Blackfoot an advantage in war. The Piegan rode south across the Rockies and drove the Shoshoni, Flathead and Kutenai off of the Plains into what is now Idaho. The Blackfeet fought any tribe that they encountered.

In the 1860's, the Piegan had animosity for the Americans. Settlers clambered onto Piegan hunting grounds. There were skirmishes between them; deaths resulted. Malcolm Clarke, a white settler, was killed by a young Piegan warrior in a family argument. The killer found refuge in the camp of Mountain Chief and the Army searched for the militants.

On January 23, 1870, Colonel Baker mistakenly attacked the peaceful camp of Piegan, under Chief Heavy Runner at dawn and massacred 173 Blackfoot Indians, called the Marias Massacre. The Militia surprised the sleeping camp, which were greatly outnumbered. Baker's militia slaughtered men, women and children. Out of 300 Indians, almost half were slain, including Chief Red Horn. nine warriors ran into the woods; most of the men were killed. The captives were mostly women and children.

Afraid that the Army was out to annihilate the Blackfoot people, many Indians fled across the Canadian border into the British possessions (Canada). The Indians called the arbitrary line dividing America and Canada the medicine line. The rest of the Piegan dwelled at that time along the Belly, Oldman and St. Mary's Rivers. The (OLD MAN) Oldman River was named after their creator god. They hunted the buffalo there and traded the skins at Fort Whoop-Up.

North of the medicine line, a battle took place between the southern Piegan and the Assiniboine tribe, allied with the Cree Indian, in northern Alberta and central Saskatchewan. The southern Piegan dwelled in northern Montana and were allied with the Blood tribe, also Blackfoot Indians. They fought near the Oldman and St. Mary's Rivers for revenge.

The Blackfoot and Cree were old enemies. At dawn, August 28, 1833, six hundred Assiniboine and Cree invaders attacked 20 lodges of Piegan camped near Fort McKenzie. They drank all night and were in no shape to fight. The Piegan had faster horses and were normally in charge. That tribe led the warriors in battle; they tried to take the first coup.

22

#9. *Apuyotsksi,* "Yellow Kidney"
(Photograph Cowtesy of Azusa Publishing, LLC)

23

Outnumbered, a messenger was sent to the Piegan main camp to reach reinforcements for help. About 500 Piegan warriors arrived and joined the battle in progress. They fought through the day and drove the Assiniboine and Cree across the medicine line, into the Bear Paw Mountains.

The Blackfeet hated the Cree. Piegan Chief White Calf's band once counted coup, scalping a Cree woman. The next morning the Bloods massacred an enemy Cree village. The Piegan fought the Cree until 1886.

One famous Blackfoot Indian chief was named Crowfoot. He led the Blackfoot in Canada after 1850. He was a great warrior and diplomat. He was a peace chief and negotiator between the Blackfoot people and the Canadian government. He fought against alcoholism in his tribe.

He adopted a Cree lad, who became Chief Poundmaker. Crowfoot was a close friend of Chief Sitting Bull. Although the Cree and the Blackfoot spoke the same language, they remained enemies. At times they were allied; other times, they fought.

Blood Chief White Calf, (*Onistapoka*), was born about 1832 and became a member of the Followers of the Buffalo band. White Calf was once called Running Crane and later was named Father of Many Children. If a Blood warrior counted coup, he could change his name.

In 1877, Piegan War-Chief White Calf led 107 of his followers, the Marrow people, to sign the Treaty of 7 to go on the reservation. He and the Blood chiefs signed the Treaty of No. 7 with the Canadian government. It called for peaceful coexistence with the Euro-Canadian immigrants and involved a 50,000 square mile region south of Red Deer River, adjacent to the Rocky Mountains. The reserve was to be located on the Bow River.
Blood Chief Red Crow was not present and did not favor the treaty. He preferred the land west of the Rocky Mountains.

The vast area controlled by the Blackfoot could be called the Land of the Blackfoot. They crossed back and forth from what is now Alberta into the land area now known as Montana over the invisible medicine line.

White Calf and Medicine Calf went back on the trail of the buffalo herds in the Montana Territory in 1879. At first, there were plenty of buffalo, but over the months, the herds depleted. Hide hunters killed buffalo by the thousands.

In the summer of 1880, the Piegan held a Sun Dance. Chiefs Bad Head Medicine Calf and White Calf sat in council with Crow Chiefs Pregnant Woman and Was Kicked and smoked the peace pipe. The Crows accepted the Piegan's gesture. The Assiniboine and Gros Ventre came in

#10. Blackfeet Peoples
Examiner.com.National

peace. From the big camp, White Calf, the Piegan hunters and the Crows went buffalo hunting if they could find the buffalo herds. Scouts rode ahead to locate the buffalo. By 1881, the buffalo disappeared from Yellowstone and the Bloods grew hungry; received no help from the Americans.

Facing starvation, Chief White Calf took leave from the Crows and led his band north to seek any buffalo herds. They rode their buffalo horses and as they approached the Bear Paw Mountains, the party heard a Blackfoot Indian singing his song of the buffalo. The Indian told them that he saw a small herd at Hairy Gap in the Little Rockies, where they located buffalo.

The hunting party mounted a hillock, where they surveyed a buffalo herd grazing across the creek. They rode in and shot many buffalo before the rest of the herd stampeded. That was the last time they would encounter buffalo. Again, White Calf's band faced starvation and had to return to Canada.

White Calf was the second war chief of the tribe under Medicine Calf, who was twenty years his senior. He was a great warrior, leader and orator. White Calf spent his time in protecting the camp and promoting native religious practices.

In the spring of 1882, White Calf's Bloods reached the reservation in southern Alberta. He had no choice but to accept government rations in the absence of buffalo. They barely survived on government beef and flour. They supplemented their diet with an occasional deer or prairie chicken they shot on the Belly River, which kept them alive. Chief White Calf prevented the reckless braves from going on the warpath and honored the treaties that he had made with the Assiniboine, Crow and Gros Ventre Indians.

In 1860, fur traders traded whiskey to them; some became drunks. In 1864, the Blackfeet caught white man's measles, causing many deaths. In 1869, smallpox killed 2,000 Blackfeet. Disease killed half their people.

In 1873, the government sponsored the wholesale slaughter of buffalo to keep the Indians on reservations; the buffalo populations dwindled down to small sporadic herds. The Indians resorted to hunting smaller game.

In 1881, a rash of mange infected their horse herds, killing one-half of the Blackfeet's horses. The buffalo were gone and the crops failed. They had little aid and suffered from alcoholism and poverty. In the winter of 1884, with severe weather, food was scarce, and the Indians starved.

Fur trappers, gold miners and settlers came west, trespassed on their lands, gave them fatal diseases and introduced dreaded alcohol to them. The American government and the Army militia took away their lands, shot their horses and forced the Blackfeet onto reservations.

Chapter Two
# Blackfeet Culture

And so it was that the Blackfoot Indians continued their journey and migrated into America. They found refuge in the Rocky Mountains and pitched their lodges there.

The Bloods and Blackfoot settled at the headwaters of the Marias and Milk Rivers, as far north as 50 degrees latitude. The Piegan tribe occupied land between the Milk and the Missouri Rivers and on the Marias and Teton Rivers. In historic times there were 50 Blackfeet bands.

The Blackfeet people believed the children of the earth were put here by *Apistokiwa* (the maker). They called themselves *Nizitapi,* (the real people). The Blackfeet also called themselves *Sukeetapi* (the prairie people). "*Apikunipuni"* means, the people.

From oral tradition, the Blackfeet transcribed a written language. A trade language spoken among Northwest Indians was pidgin. Plains Indians used a universal sign language to understand different dialects.

Sign language was used to surprise the enemy during warfare. Hunters used sign language to surprise their prey. It was also used to negotiate treaties with Indians and to make peace between Indian tribes. It was the universal language. The hand signs were very effective.

The Blackfeet was a tribe who utilized sign talking. A stranger might have held up the first two fingers held together, for friend. The sign for dirt was to point down to the earth and to rub the fingers together. The sign for mountain was to raise the right fist straight above the head, then sign hard, striking the left palm with the right hand three times.

Kiowa Indians are noted for originating the sign language. They were the most prolific sign talkers on the Plains, along with the Teton Dakota (Sioux). The American Indian sign language is still used today, primarily at ceremonies, festivals and intertribal powwows. Other forms of communication that were utilized were ponies and mirrors as well as smoke signals, where wet blankets were used over a bonfire.

Plains Indians used buffalo and other large skins to paint scenes. Paintings depicted battle, hunting or other displays using symbols, recorded in posterity. Pictographs were ancient drawings or paintings using symbols to represent animal and human figures etched on stones, stone walls and caves and could indicate a camp, landmark, or meeting place.

Algonquians were of eight major language groupings in America. There were three main family language groups: the Central, Eastern and Plains tribes. The Arapaho, Blackfeet and Cheyenne were Algonquian speakers of the Plains group. The Algonquian speakers included Arapaho, Cheyenne, Chippewa, Cree, Delaware, Fox, Mohican, Powhatan and Shawnee as well as many other tribes.

The Blackfeet tongue is a sing-song musical dialect, with complicated verbs and lengthy words to pronounce. An exception is *oki*, their word for hello. Man is *"ninii;"* woman is *"aakii."* Sun is *"ki'somm"* and water is *"aokii."* There is no word for goodbye in the Blackfeet language. The Blackfeet tongue remains the most aberrant dialect of the Algonquian stock; possibly because of separation.

The band was the basic unit in the political grouping that formed the tribe; some bands were residential composite groups. They had to be willing to be led. The famous archeologist, Wissler, described the band as instinctive and physical. Other bands were formed of extended families and territorially based governed by a council of leaders who directed the tribal affairs.

Smaller bands lived in encampments while larger bands formed villages. The camp circle was used on a move for security. Bands scattered in winter to mountain stream valleys protected from the wind. Deer, grouse, rabbit, sage hen and quail were hunted for sustenance. They also fished.

The headman was the band leader or band chief. These categories or groupings might be broken down into war leader, hunt leader, etc. The band leader was picked by election and not by residence or kinship. He had to be a good warrior and generous. The death of a band leader caused the band to shift and the band disbanded to form again. So, they moved their camp.

The word, "chief" was synonymous with headman. Tribal head chiefs were popular for cooperating with the tribe. When the tribal head chief called a council, he summoned the headmen of the bands and societal chiefs. He relied on persuasion to lead the tribe. When family bands were combined in a village or winter camp, they had a headman. His role was social director of ceremonies, dances, festivals, hunts and war.

The council was a delegation of band chiefs; one headman represented each society, called by the tribal head chief. Important matters of the tribe were discussed by the council. They discussed following the buffalo and ceremonial hunts. The will of the tribal council was decided by consensus or a vote. The crier was a leader who broadcasted and made the announcements of the council to the band. He was known as a herald.

The Blackfeet peoples had clans or gens. Clans were named for an animal totem, for instance, coyote or turtle. They refused to kill the animal of their totem. Members of a clan were from one ancestor and came into a clan through familial relations. Some followed through their father's clan. Others may have joined the mother's clan. A taboo was that members of the same clan could not marry, extending into the band, and to never marry a relative. Marrying outside of the clan is called exogamy. Exogamy was practiced religiously until historic times when taboos were relaxed and the wife and children belonged to the husband's band. Bands were loosely organized and a man was able to join his wife's band.

Medicine men were persons in the tribe who had exhibited supernatural powers through dreams and visions. The Blackfeet medicine man was the spiritual leader of the tribe and a man of mystery and magic.

Medicine men led medicine bands who assisted him in warding off evil and healing illness. His healing was masked with mysticism and secrecy. The medicine man's mystery was of a sacred nature. He had powers through his magic to forecast and heal maladies. Superstition and fear surrounded the medicine shaman. The shaman made his own medicine before important events like moving camp and going on the war trail.

The shaman used magic, charms, fans, fetishes and sometimes peyote (a hallucinatory drug) to perform his feats. Sacred items, like an eagle claw, feather or bone were utilized. The Medicine man gained power by healing the sick using herbs or other methods. Herbs used in healing were bear grass, Crow root, parsnip, juniper and sweet sage. He used drums, medicine, bone whistles, gourd rattles, an animal bladder filled with pebbles or deer hoof rattles, chants, prayers and incantations to heal.

The Medicine man communicated with the spirit world through visions. During such a vision, he might go into a trance to perform healing. When he came out of his trance, the shaman would give an auricle. A medicine man could claim to suck poison and illness out of a patient. He would then spit out the evil spirit on the ground. A twisted piece of sweet grass was burned and the smoke was fanned to induce cleansing.

As the Blackfeet medicine man donned a yellow bear skin, he became the bear and emulated the bruin. The shaman claimed to receive the bear's spirit, which is called ceremonial transformation. He was respected and feared and had powers to charm antelope and buffalo during the hunt.

The sacred rite-of-passage for a young brave or maiden during puberty was the vision quest, a religious experience directly related to their Sun god. The brave ventured out alone into the wild and remained there until he received his vision. He or she usually chose a mountainside close to the gods, and the young maiden might choose a hill or safer environment.

The vision quest was a religious ordeal conducted in nature for a young man or woman to receive a spiritual revelation. Much preparation for the quest involved fasting and prayer to seek the desired divination. Self-purification by bathing, fanning the sweet grass smoke or sage towards oneself, personal sacrifice and taking sweat baths induced purity.

A medicine robe was crafted from newly tanned skin and painted with white clay or a medicine bundle was taken on the ordeal. Young braves or girls began their quest before the age of ten and visions did not always come. A little known fact was that some female Blackfeet actually became women warriors and rode the war trail. Interpreting a vision sometimes resulted in lament. The experience could never be fabricated.

Animals and nature played a big role in their belief system. He or she fasted in the wild for several days of isolation; the person could experience a supernatural vision from nature in the form of a bear, eagle, magpie or wolf spirit as their totem, for example. If an eagle appeared, one might take a new name, like Striking Eagle. If the quest was successful, the young brave or woman achieved his or her spirit guide through life that would give the seeker a new name, medicine or powers. A feather or claw of the animal was used as a personal fetish and placed in his medicine bundle; an offering song might be sung to the Sun god.

A young man was called a brave and after battle was considered a warrior. He was taught early to hunt with a rabbit stick, like a boomerang and became proficient with a bow and arrow; he could then hunt for food. A brave needed to have success on the battlefield to qualify for marriage.

The Blackfeet were polygamous, like the Shoshoni and other Plains tribes. The groom took the bride's sisters as wives. Men normally afforded one wife. It seemed to be a question of economics. Five wives were the usual maximum if a man had wealth. One extreme example was one Blackfeet man who had five wives, 22 sons and five daughters. Some very affluent males had as many as seven wives.

A man's first wife was the head wife. She was referred to as one who sits beside him. Her sisters were called distant wives, until they joined him and were then called real wives. If the bride elected, she could choose the groom's brothers as her husband's and if a man died, his wife would marry his brother(s). This is called a levirate relationship.

When Blackfeet girls came of age, usually around twelve years old, a marriage was consummated. They practiced arranged marriages. Males past puberty would hang around where the young women drew water, carried wood and near their teepees at night. If a young man fell in love with a girl, his parents made the proposal. On occasion, the girl simply followed her suitor to his parents' lodge.

Blackfeet women were not promiscuous. Chastity was a virtue. There were harsh penalties for acts of infidelity, a taboo. The husband might kill his wife if she was unfaithful. She might be branded for life. Marriage customs dictated purity over immorality and the sanctity of marriage. Young women did not associate with men. The girl left her parent's clan and married into a new clan. If she lived in the groom's father's lodge at first, the practice was referred to as patrilocal. It was forbidden to marry in the same clan to avoid marrying blood relatives. The bride then identified with the clan of her in-laws. Sexual beginnings were foretold in their mythology.

If the girl's parent's picked a son-in-law for their daughter, the girl's father would suggest that she carry food to his lodge for one month (moon). At the time of her engagement, her parents were expected to gift his family with moccasins decorated with dyed porcupine quills. The groom doubled any gifts from the bride. A feast was prepared by the bride's parents for his relatives. The bride and her mother carried the food and moccasins to his lodge for the feast; the mother of the bride had to remain outside, because of taboos. The son-in-law could not look at his mother-in-law.

If the young couple's lodge was next to her parent's lodge, her father built their morning fire and her mother brought their meals, but it was taboo to enter their lodge, as per custom. The mother could have no dealings with the son-in-law. This was called avoidance. If the son-in-law appeared in his mother-in-law's presence, it was a breach of custom and caused her shame. To make amends, he had to present her with a horse. The mother could visit her daughter only if her husband was not home.

The girl's mother was to prepare a new lodge as a gift to the newlyweds. She furnished the lodge with blankets, mountain lion skins, buffalo robes, parfletch pouches, and a buckskin dress for the bride with a buckskin suit for the groom. She saved the lodge until the band migrated to a new camp site to pitch the lodge for the newlyweds. The father' job was to provide the lodge decoration. The new groom and his father-in-law could

#11. Plainswoman, Horse and Travois
(Photograph Courtesy of Jumper Horse/Sport

have dealings and be the best of friends. The bride's father was to gift the couple with 30 or 40 horses. The groom in turn, gave his father-in law the same number of horses, his best buffalo horse and war bonnet as a "bride price" or "bride wealth."

Bride wealth was gifts given to a woman's family by the husband and his kinsmen. Kinship is the complex system of intimate relationships arising from marriage and descent.

Divorce was not common, but occurred occasionally. If a woman was lazy or caught in adultery, she was divorced. The husband, on the other hand, might be abandoned for cruelty or neglect. Women were traded, brides and mothers. The order of importance to the Blackfeet Indian was family, community, tribe and society.

The wickiup was a cone-shaped hut with upright poles, similar to the tipi. This conical hut was covered with bark, brush, or matting. Rabbit or buffalo fur blankets kept them warm in the winter plus heated rocks were placed under foot to keep them cozy. The willow hut or thatch hut was similar in construction to the brush hut. Prior to the tipi, a similar dwelling was constructed of long willow poles, tied at the top in a conical configuration. The framework was covered with sewn matting of tule reeds or other thatch. Brush huts were similar in construction to the wickiup with upright poles tied near the top and sagebrush or branches for covering.

Huts were used for special events. A menstrual hut was one such dwelling. When an Indian girl came of age, she began menstruation. She spent the time of her menses in a hut.

After the baby was born it was named weeks later, when the father paid a prominent member of the tribe to name the child. The name might have been for a brave deed of the person naming. Nicknames were often applied. Sometimes, a prominent person requested that a communal sweat lodge be built where prayers were offered for the infant. Blackfeet women carried the babies in cradleboards decorated with colored glass seed beads on their backs, while they worked and raised the children.

Communal sweat lodges were used by the men to socialize. Sweat baths were followed by a plunge into cold water. The Blackfeet walled up running hot springs with stones to make a permanent hot tub. Natural spring water contained minerals healthy for the body. The Indians built sweat lodges, used by the men to socialize. The sweat baths were followed by a cold plunge.

#12. Glacial Teepee
(Photograph Courtesy of Azusa Publishing, LLC)

The Blackfeet Indians were hunters and gatherers like other Plains Indian tribes and had division among the sexes. Men hunted and women gathered. Men used bow and arrows to shoot antelope, bear, buffalo, cougar, deer, large birds, moose, mountain sheep, rabbit and other animals for food. Arrows were marked to identify the bearer. A color stripe or a number of stripes were employed. A red mark on the feather could have been used. The Indians killed deer from hunting blinds constructed in a circle using large boulders. The walls acted as a blind to shoot deer with bow and arrows. Remnants of these blinds still exist today in the Northwest.

After the atlatl came the bow and arrow in the last 2,000 years. The men hunted game with bow and arrows. Fathers taught their sons early on how to use the bow and arrow. The Blackfeet Indians crafted fine bows and arrows of cedar, juniper, oak, osage and yew. The bows were made of ash wood and sinew backed in a straight style, about four feet in length. Animal skin was wrapped around bows for fortification; often, rattlesnake skin was used, partially for adornment. Bowstrings were made from animal gut (sinew).

A shaft was heated and straightened, smoothed and polished for an arrow. Indians flint knapped (chipped) arrowheads from chert or obsidian and inserted them into a slit at the end of the shaft. Arrows were crafted of service berry or willow, tipped with stone, bone or wood arrow points. Stone arrowheads were normally flaked from chert. It was glued with pitch and wrapped with sinew. Eagle, hawk or similar feathers were used to fletch an arrow.

Quivers of cougar or otter skin held their arrows. War shields and armor were made of tough buffalo hide to deflect arrows. Personal symbols appeared on war shields, teepees and clothing. The warrior was equipped with a lance, bow and arrows, war-club, war shield and knife.

#13. Horse Atsina War party
(Photograph Courtesy of Azusa Publishing, LLC)

Prehistoric knives were flaked from chert, with a bone or wooden handle. Historic knives bartered from fur trade forts were steel with leather sheathes that were beaded. Scalp knives were wooden handled butcher knives traded from forts.

Tomahawks and war clubs normally had wooden handles and were monolithic (with a deep groove), or flaked heads were hafted on with strips of rawhide. Ball clubs were a large round stone sewn into leather with a strap, swung around the head. Stone hammers were similarly made. Tomahawk pipes had English, French or Spanish trade-blades adorned with beaded pendants. The instrument had a dual purpose as a pipe to be smoked or a weapon for war.

Native Americans in America were of the stone-age. Lithic tools were made of antler, bone, horn, stone, wood and fastened with sinew. Stone tools were very popular. Adzes, arrowheads, awls, drill points, gravers, hide scrapers, knives and shaft scrapers were flint-knapped (chipped) from basalt, chert or obsidian. Tomahawks were monolithic or flaked from stone. Hand axes, root diggers and shovels were fashioned of larger cores.

They were a nation of hunter-warriors. The American Indians groomed the forests using starter fires to burn off dead wood and brush. Game was killed sparingly in order to eliminate waste. Meat was consumed, practicing good ecology of the region.

The Blackfeet women performed the menial chores, while the men did the hunting and defended the camp. Before the hunt, the men sang the hunting songs. Females carried water and fetched firewood. Women tended the fires. Pine-nuts, greens, small animals, and turtles were gathered for food. The females foraged for seeds and dug camas. The main root consumed by the Blackfeet Indians was the camas root.

The roots were dug in autumn, utilizing sticks or stone diggers. They were gathered in bulk before digging a large pit, much like the Bannock. Stones were placed on the bottom of the pit and a fire was set ablaze in it. When the fire burned down, willow branches were placed over the piping hot stones. The camas root was then placed on the branches. Dirt was piled over the camas roots. A fire was started on top of the earth to form an oven. The women tended the fire for a 36-hour period until the cooking task was done. The camas was eaten, stored or ground in mortars into flour or meal to make camas bread.

#14. Young Piegan Warrior
(Photograph Courtesy of Azusa Publishing, LLC)

Wild fruits and vegetables were gathered by the women. Wild celery, onions, potatoes, and turnips were garnered. Women dug camas and dozens of other edible roots and underground parts. Prickly pear was a favorite fruit. They foraged and gathered berries, cherries, fleshy fruits, leaves, nuts, other fruits and seeds; while the men hunted game.

Women cooked for the family, cared for the children and made the clothing and owned the belongings inside the tipi. They used caches, pits dug in the ground and lined with rocks to store food and other possessions. Sometimes, pre-forms and arrowheads were stashed this way for later use. Other women's duties were to gather firewood and water.

Fire was produced from friction, by rubbing a fire stick between the palms or by the use of a bow drill and a wooden shaft held by a drill cup.

Plant fibers were used to make cordage in the manufacture of bags, netting and rope. They made log rafts, lashed together. Reed rafts were constructed that were light enough for their women to tote on their backs.

The Blackfeet were nomadic and not sedentary. Evidence of pottery and basketry making has not been found. Baskets and pottery were garnered through trade. This tradition was practiced by more stationary tribes. Referral to the traditional art of making earthenware by their ancestors is uncharacteristic of the nomadic buffalo hunters, according to Lowie.

Bones were broken up in mortars for the marrow. Bison and mountain sheep horn made spoons; hooves made glue to fletch arrows and attach arrowheads. Bone made awls, burins and needles for sewing; sinew made bindings and bowstrings. Their handicraft was ingenious.

Indian women scraped the hides and rubbed them with animal brains. The skin was chewed, pounded in mortars, kneaded and stretched to make it pliable. Since rawhide hardens after becoming wet, the Indians utilized a smoking method instead. A pit was dug and a fire started, using white cedar. The skin was laid out over bent green willows and hung over the fire, making sure that the fire did not blaze and ruin the skin.

Indian buckskin was made using a different procedure and not tanned. Smoking the leather made the finished product soft and supple, and was often used in women's clothing. It was easily cut and sewed and could be washed. The skin could then be dyed red, using wild peach bark or yellow-red, utilizing a solution of boiled red oak bark.

The Blackfeet were Plains Indians and wore the full regalia. Their garb was made from soft deerskin. Women tanned hides and made all of the clothing that they wore using awls, bone eye needles and gut for sewing.

Women wore dresses and jackets of deerskin or trade-cloth. Both sexes wore leggings. Women's leggings were worn snug fitting to the knee, either wrapped or buttoned. The women donned deerskin or elk dresses (adorned with porcupine quills), with fringes and a belt. In the heat of summer they wore skirts, with the breasts exposed, with deer skin leggings from the moccasins to the knees. Young children remained naked until they were around six.

The men wore breech clouts (loin cloths), deerskin war-shirts (tunics) and moccasins. Leggings reached from the hips to the ankles (bare at the buttocks) and extended past the seams and were fringed. Leggings were decorated with beadwork, quillwork or painted designs.

Moccasins were crafted by different methods. A unique Plains moccasin type was the hock moccasin. This leather was formed from the sheath of the hock section from the foreleg of the deer, made from one piece, with the hair on the inside. The top was sewn shut and fitted with a leather thong to tie it. Another way was to form them from three pieces of leather obtained from the upper leg sheath of the deer. This method was called the Freemont style. Soft soles were worn in winter and hard soles in summer.

The Blackfeet, like the Sioux, dyed porcupine quills bright colors using plant pigments to decorate moccasins and leggings in unique geometric patterns. After the arrival of the Hudson's Bay Company, the Blackfeet adorned their moccasins with tiny bright colored glass seed beads that might cover them and dyed them black.

A combination of finite glass beads and quills were used. The Blackfeet could be recognized by the three-prong design beaded on their moccasins indicating the three Blackfoot tribes.

In winter, bearskin, buffalo or rabbit fur robes were worn. The robes could be worn for cozy outer wear in the winter cold. Buffalo sleeping robe blankets made frigid winters tolerable. Buffalo robes worn as an outer garment kept them warm in cold weather. Trade-blankets were worn after the coming of the white man. A blanket Indian was an Indian that refused to accept the ways of the white man. He wore only the blanket in protest.

Women wore their long hair loose with a head band or tied in thick braids tied with otter fur strips. The men wore their hair loose with a forelock that hung to the nose or braids. Medicine Pipe men rolled their hair into a thick topknot, held with clay above the forehead. Indians wore bear oil in their hair. They adorned their hair with beads, feathers and fur. Hair brushes were made of porcupine quills or horse hair with a rawhide handle.

A brave usually wore one feather in his hair. Feathers had meaning. Worn to the rear meant he had been wounded in battle. A split feather designated that he had been wounded. A notched red feather showed that he had taken a scalp. During winter, the braves wore leather caps made of badger, coyote or otter fur, adorned with feathers or dyed porcupine quills.

A hole was drilled through a bear tooth and a thong was strung through it. A number of teeth strung together would make a bear tooth necklace. Elk teeth were sewn onto their garments for decoration. After the white man came, the Indians took tobacco tin lids and fashioned them into bell shaped decorations, hundreds were sewn on to fancy Indian dresses.

It was the custom of the Plains Indians to capture live eaglets and raise them to full growth for use of their feathers for war bonnets. The Blackfoot manufactured stick cages of tree branches secured with sinew to house the eagles. By caging the eagles, it was not necessary to kill such a magnificent bird for their feathers. Live eagles were kept to supply beautiful feathers to craft their war bonnets. Wings of large birds made fans and the down made ornate decorations on pipes, prayer sticks shields, and wands.

Another method was to trap mature eagles and finish them off for the same purpose. A pit was dug deep enough to house a man near the foot of the mountains, where eagles were plentiful. The pit was covered with green branches and grasses. The catcher crawled below and baited the trap with a fresh killed coyote or buffalo meat. When the eagle dove down to grasp the bait, the catcher grabbed its legs, pulling the bird down and wrang its neck. He waited there from dawn to dark, having prayed, chanted eagle songs and rubbed himself with sweet sage smoke to free his body of scent. He left the pit after several eagles were caught, to provide enough meat, feathers for bonnets and eagle bones for whistles. Golden eagle feather was preferred...

A complete war-bonnet was worthy of a chief, who normally wore them. These headdresses were tubular. The war bonnet consisted of a buckskin cap for the crown, with a strip sewn to it. The entire bonnet was bedecked with eagle feathers. They had ermine tails hanging from the sides and bits of colored cloth fastened to adorn the bonnet. Others had eagle feather war bonnets that trailed all the way to the ground. The long feather train represented the back of the buffalo. A feather was added to the headband for each act of bravery. A coup counted as one feather on a war bonnet. War bonnets were distinctive to each tribe. A war bag included a parfleche case that contained the war-bonnet and extra cartridges for battle. Trade guns bartered to the Indians were flintlocks, muskets and pistols.

In the village, the men and boys went down to the river to bathe, as a daily routine. The women had a similar routine for communal bathing. For purity, the men took steam baths. It was how the men socialized. A cold plunge might have followed into a lake or river, or they laid down nude and rolled around in the snow as another method of keeping fit.

A warrior would stand outside of his teepee and shout an invitation to his friends and elders to come to his lodge for feast and smoke. With everyone seated, the women served buffalo tongue, ribs pemmican and stewed berries. They sat around the campfire and told stories of battle and the hunt with laughter and sang songs and chanted.

The Blackfeet had feasts, when food was plentiful, given for relatives and friends. After a successful hunt was a good time for the feast. The celebration and feasting could go on for days, until all of the guests left. Some feasts were only for men. Others sacrificed bones from the meal in the fire to the gods. The feast was a time for dancing, feasting, prayers, songs and storytelling.

After the feast, as they sat around the campfire, the host would cut leaves to be smoked in a calumet pipe, which was popular. Hand-crafted pipes were made of clay or stone. A mixture of tobacco, bearberry, leaves or a bark and tobacco mixture was called kinnikinnick. Tobacco root grew wild or was planted. Later, tobacco was traded from the forts.

The host filled his pipe, took a burning twig from the fire and lit it. He inhaled the sweet aroma and passed the pipe. It was smoked and passed east to west in the path of the sun. The pipe was raised to their gods, the Sun, Moon and Stars, uttering a prayer and was passed around to his guests, until all had smoked the pipe. The pipe was smoked for ceremonies, pleasure, good luck and in friendship. The peace pipe was also smoked to bind treaties. It was a tranquil time to talk. The host cleaned the pipe when it was smoked out by tapping it on the cutting board. He would then say, "It is burned out," and the guests left.

Blackfeet children loved to hunt with their fathers. Little girls had dolls with deerskin dresses. The boys and girls loved to play games. La Cross was a popular game played with a deerskin ball and hooped sticks with netting across them. The ball was driven to the goal. Chunky was a game played with crooked sticks to roll a stone disk to the goal. The game of hands, the hoop game and ring toss were played. Bone or stone dice were played for betting, thrown into a wooden bowl. The youth sang and played games with clay or stone game pieces, like button, button who has the button?  Game stones were lagged to a line or thrown to hit the other stone. Youths loved to Indian-wrestle, run foot races and race their ponies

Both genders engaged in storytelling, artwork and music.  Songs and dancing were much a part of the Blackfeet society.  Legends were conveyed by oral tradition.  Stories were told to all.  Incantation and songs were passed from generation to generation.  The Blackfeet were known for their fine beadwork, embroidery and quillwork.

The prehistoric Blackfeet believed in the underwater gods.  A very old Blackfeet Indian legend told of the Under Water Persons, (*Su'-ye-tu'-pi*) in their personification that ate people and fish.  They believed that if they took from the *Su'yetu'pi*; they would take from them.  Because of their beliefs in that legend and the fact that the Blackfeet preferred buffalo meat to fish might explain their distaste for fish.

The Blackfeet, Crow and Comanche regarded fish as taboo.  The nomadic Blackfeet Indians were accustomed to follow the buffalo herds.  I asked a Blackfeet elder why his people did not eat fish.  He had asked his uncle that question.  His answer was, "too many bones."

The famed archeologist, Robert Lowie, contended that the Blackfeet fished in times of need, but because of the movement of the buffalo hunters he thought that it was contradicted.

Musical instruments were hand crafted.  Wooden rasps, played with a stick, were made from sagebrush.  Wooden hoops covered with skin and tied on the back, served as a drum.  A section of hollow log with a skin head made a tom-tom.  Flutes were carved from wood; medicine whistles were crafted of bone from eagle wings.  Everything that the Indian needed he crafted from nature.  The American Indian life-style was self-sustaining and very industrious.

#15. American Bison by Curtis
(Photograph Courtesy of Azusa Publishing, LLC)

## Chapter Three
### Horse and Buffalo People

Blackfeet Indians formed a powerful buffalo hunting society. Their culture centered on the buffalo, horse and warfare. The Blackfeet bands of the Northwestern Plains were nomads, since they followed the movements of the buffalo herds by the weather and season. They moved their villages with the bison migration constantly during the spring, summer and fall. Bands of 20 to 30 families comprising possibly of 150 men, women and children of extended families led by a head man or hunt leader followed the buffalo. Buffalo provided much needed meat, skins, clothing, moccasins, horns, tools and teepee coverings. Their diet was predominately buffalo meat, an excellent staple. A favorite meal was buffalo meat and berries.

Buffalo were believed to have been created just for the Indian people. Buffalo horns and hooves were used in religious ceremonies. The Plains Indians depended on the buffalo for sustenance, lodging, robes, items of clothing and other bi-products. The Blackfeet were successful hunters and provided food for their people. They had enough jerky and pemmican left over for the traders at the forts. Buffalo were hunted for their skins and robes. The Indians engaged in trapping and hunting animals for the furs or hides used in trade. Antelope, bear, beaver, buffalo, deer, elk, fox and wolf made good skins or robes.

The Plains Indians believed the buffalo to be sacred. It completed their life style. A rare, one in a million species, was the white buffalo. The rare bison was eulogized by the people of the Plains. Many stories in legends were told of the white buffalo, which was a phenomenon.

The buffalo roamed within a large triangle between Great Bear Lake, in Canada in the Northwest, south into Mexico, and eastward along the Appalachian Mountains. There was an abundance of bison on the Snake River Plain westward into Oregon, to the base of the Blue Mountains before the turn of the 19th Century. The buffalo had disappeared due to over-kill.

The buffalo was the mammal hunted in the largest land volume by Indians. It was estimated that at one time there were 50,000,000 buffalo on the Plains west of the Mississippi. After the government decree to slaughter the buffalo there was a scarcity of bison on the Snake River Plains, hunters had to travel to the Upper Missouri to find the buffalo. In 1860, an estimate was that there were 3,000,000 buffalo left on the American Plains.

Wild buffalo originally roamed free on the Snake River Plain as far west as the Blue Mountains, in what is now Oregon. Buffalo were the largest mammals in America. Buffalo ranged in smaller herds, but grazed in massive herds in the summer, during mating season. Buffalo were some of the largest mammals in America. The Woodland buffalo is the world's largest cattle species. The buffalo has a shaggy coat in winter but a lighter summer coat. Bison reach six to ten feet in length and weigh more than a ton. Despite their size, buffalo run, reaching speeds of forty miles per hour.

Older bison were more dominant. Their age created a hierarchy. Males tended to be larger and dominant bulls. Dominant males passed on their dominance by breeding early in the season and being most fertile. Buffalo herds are made up of bulls, cows and calves, like cattle. Female buffalo roamed in maternal herds, including male and female offspring. Males left the herd around three years of age to roam alone or join a bachelor herd. Male and female bison herds migrated in season for annual grasses and mixed only during mating season. Males fought for mating rites.

Bison are grazing ruminants that feed on grasses, sedges, and berries and lichen. They ate grasses in little time and had to migrate to reach other grasses. They used their head and horns to clear vegetation of snow.

Buffalo are quite gregarious and usually ranged in smaller herds, but grazed in massive herds in the summer, during mating season. Buffalo are polygamous in the mating season. Bulls fight to breed the cows. Dominant bulls maintain their harem in season. A bull tended his estrous cow by following her around until she accepted him. He would stand and shield her eyes from a challenging bull. If the challenger bellowed, the tending bull would answer. Dominant bulls most mated within the first two to three weeks. Submissive males mated with estrous cows not mated.

Walking Blackfeet located the roving American bison herds in the wild for the hunt. The hunters first approached the herd from downwind, so as to not alert the herd of their presence. They had to be very careful not to scare the buffalo and cause a stampede, which was quite dangerous. A certain number of Plains Indians lost their lives after being gored by maddened buffaloes. Buffalo hunting took skill. Crawling among the wild buffalo, concealed under a wolf skin, a hunter could stalk a buffalo and get a clean shot with a bow and arrow. At times, a decoy buffalo was used.

Cow buffalo were taken in November, prior to the cold season. As the Blackfeet continued to hunt the buffalo, the herd began drifting farther and farther away. They were slaughtered before winter in order to make robes before the cold season. The hunters butchered the bison and the women stretched the hides and staked them down. The Blackfeet ate red meat primarily, but ate some fowl and little or no fish. They worked arduously to scrape the hides and remove all of the flesh and fat with stone hide scrapers. Fleshed robes were tanned using bison brains.

Fresh meat was cooked in a stew or roasted on a spit. The excess meat was made into jerky and saved for winter. Buffalo meat, deer or elk was jerked and finally ground in a mortar and pestle or a buffalo skin mortar and mano to nearly a powder. The bison meal was mixed with animal fat and chokecherries, ground in a mortar and pestle, and made into cakes or placed in bags, called pemmican, which was stored underground for winter. Woven bags were sewn out of sagebrush fibers and used to store foods underground.

Meat was cooked in clay vessels, a paunch (the belly of an animal and its contents), rawhide vessels, water baskets lined with pitch, or in a pit. Water was boiled in a paunch or skin held with four stakes in the ground and hot rocks added to heat. Women did the cooking and preparation. An inventive method of cooking was with red-hot stones heated in a fire. They were transferred into a water-basket, sealed with pitch. As the water simmered, meat was added to cook. Spits over the fire were used for broiling meat. The fire-dog (three slender flat rocks supported a pot over a fire).

In the cold of winter, with deep snows and howling headwinds, the roving bison found refuge in wooded valleys and hilly terrain, giving refuge from the wind. Bison wintered in timber where the snow was shallow. The used their scruffy coarse fur faces to brush away the snow to make a clearing to lie down. Heavy snows slowed them and they became easy targets for Indian hunter's arrows. Snow shoes were worn on these occasions. Their structural movement has been referred to as the seasonal round. Before the horse, the Blackfeet located the herds of buffalo on foot. Wolves often followed the herds and attacked buffalo in packs. Buffalo were accustomed to lone wolves being in the vicinity, who were not a danger to them.

One hunting method was the buffalo surround. They formed a large circle surrounding a herd of wild buffalo. The hunters moved in, closing the circle as they fired arrows into the beasts and then slaughtered them.

The buffalo corral (pound) was constructed in a V shape, on a down slope. The shaman would crawl among the herd beneath a buffalo robe. He would bleat like a baby buffalo as he moved. Buffalo have poor eyesight anyway, and the dumb animals would follow him into the corral and become entrapped, where they were shot with bow and arrows.

The Blackfeet tribe employed the buffalo jump method to hunt bison. The buffalo jump was a communal undertaking where the buffaloes killed were shared by the tribe. Lanes were built on a cliff adjoining a bluff using rock barriers along the sides forming a kind of runway. The medicine man might start a fire or just whoop and wave a blanket near a herd grazing near the cliff to spook and stampede them over the edge. Processing stations below were utilized to butcher the bison for the meat and to remove the hides. The band shared the meat of the buffalo, and there was little waste.

Before the horse, the Blackfeet bands used domestic dogs and travois to haul goods, meat, hides, jerky and other goods. They hauled moderate loads until the horse. This was the only method the Indians had to transport goods for hundreds of years. Dogs were kept as pets and watchdogs. There was a story of an enemy Indian tribe that attacked a village during the night and massacred the camp. The dogs slept and failed to bark and warn them of the attack. The dogs were slain and hung from a tree as a reminder.

Certain tribes ate the meat of young tender puppies. The Arapaho and Cheyenne allies of the Blackfeet ate dog meat. This practice was looked down on by some tribes. The dog was sacred to the Blackfeet.

A horse, similar to the Appaloosa, appeared on a cave painting in France in 15,000 B.P. The ancient horse disappeared in America. The Moors had horses when they conquered Spain in 800 A.D. The Spanish overthrew the Moors in 1,400 A.D., but retained their horses and Spanish Mustangs. In 1493, Spanish Mustangs were aboard of Columbus' sailing vessel, bound for America. When Cortez landed on the shore of the Gulf of Mexico in 1519, his ship carried horses for his cavalry.

Conquistadores from Europe invaded American shores with delusions of finding gold in the Americas. They were followed by Spanish colonists, who landed on the Pacific Coast of Mexico and California. With them, they brought the first modern horses to America. Cortez brought ten stallions and six mares in 1519. Mustangs escaped from the colonists' ranches and soon wild feral horse herds roamed the deserts of the Southwest. These horses were later named the American Mustang. The Spaniards continued to transport horses on their vessels. Many horses escaped and became wild or feral horses and formed herds in the American Southwest.

Ute Indians stole horses from the Spanish in the 1500s during night raids or caught wild horses in the desert. Legends tell us that when they first saw horses, the Ute Indians thought that they were big dogs. The Blackfeet called them elk dogs. The Comanche named them god dogs and the Sioux used the term, "medicine dogs". The Utes became the first horse-mounted American Indians. Stories were told of man and rider being as one creature.

Cortez made slaves of any horse thieves that they found among the Ute Indians and forced them to work in their gold mines. Spanish conquistadors imprisoned the Pueblo Indians. The Spanish mistreated the Apache and Navaho slaves. They treated the slaves very poorly. Sometimes they were killed. When 211 Navahos were captured while celebrating and taken prisoner, only 35 were released. They were getting restless.

Then, in the mid or late 1600's, the Spanish colonists and the Ute Indians came to an agreement for the Slave Trade. The Utes went on raids of neighboring tribes, like the Bannock, Shoshoni and Navaho, kidnapping women and children for slaves that they traded to the colonists for horses. They were made house slaves to the Spanish colonists. A female slave, for instance, traded for eight horses. The Ute became a very wealthy tribe.

Navajos who had been enslaved as common servants in the Pueblos rebelled. The Indians overthrew the Spanish rule, called the Pueblo Revolt of 1680, in northeastern New Mexico. The Indians rose up and pushed the Spanish colonists out that year. Many were killed. The colonists fled the country. In their haste, they left thousands of horses behind. Hundreds of horses were there for the taking. In the early 1700's, horses made their appearance on the Plains. The Indians garnered many horses at that time.

An ancient Indian trail, later known as the Old Spanish Trail, provided a gateway for Ute and Navaho raiders to steal horses from the California rancheros. It was also utilized by the Ute traders during the Slave Trade. Routes ran north-south in the upper Rio Grande Valley, between the pueblos in now New Mexico and the San Luis Valley (in what is now Colorado). The route became the west fork of the north branch.

Apache Indians stole horses from the colonists, while the Comanche Indians counted coup by stealing horses from the Apache. They trailed horses north for trade with their Shoshoni relatives and the American Indian Horse Culture began early, circa 1700. They traded horses at the Shoshoni-held trade fairs.

Boise River Shoshoni were one of the first Snake bands to acquire horses. Their horses grazed on the plush green grasses of the Boise River bottoms called Peace Valley, where there was good drinking water. The Nez Perce also acquired the Appaloosa horse, most likely from the Comanche Indians. This horse became the favorite breed of the Nez Perce. The Ute, Apache and Comanche were the first American Indians to acquire horses.

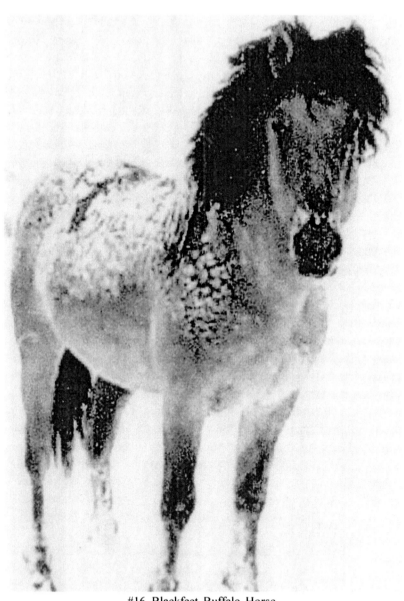

#16. Blackfeet Buffalo Horse
Photo courtesy ofwww.aaanativearts.com

The Plains horse complex diffused to tribes throughout the Northwest. According to legend, the first time that the Blackfeet Indians saw horses, the Shoshoni were riding them in an attack on their village. The Shoshoni had the advantage until the Blackfeet, also had the horse. The trade fairs held in Shoshoni territory, in what is now Idaho attracted Bannocks, Crows, Flatheads and Nez Perce to trade with the Shoshonis. They had fine horses to barter. The Rocky Mountain Fur Company met with them to exchange trade goods. The Boise Shoshoni and the Eastern Shoshoni Indians held an annual Trade Fair and traded horses in the autumn.

Legend tells us that Blackfeet war parties rode south for hundreds of miles, reaching the Spanish colonies in what became New Mexico Territory for horses. They stole hundreds of Spanish Cayuses. They were gone over a two-year period, before arriving in Blackfeet Country, trailing stolen horses. It was not long before they had built up good sized herds of horses.

The Blackfeet Indians journeyed to Mexico and returned with a large string of horses, including the Spanish Mustang. They picked these sturdy ponies as their buffalo horses. They probably had the Spanish Mustang early. They were a medium-sized pony, measuring 14 hand spans (6") at the front shoulder. Their average weight was around 1,000 pounds.

The Old North Trail ran south from present day Calgary on the eastern slope of the Rocky Mountains, straight south, not encompassing the hills or mountains, to where Helena now stands, southward reaching into Mexico. An aged Piegan chief, Brings-Down–the-Sun described Piegan war parties returning on the trail in 1787 with horses stolen in Mexico.

The Blackfeet captured a magnificent black stallion, but it broke loose, escaped and became a killer. It stole mares for his herd and caused great destruction of property. The animal was like a phantom running and plundering at night. Its blue black coat was unseen in the darkness; its mane and tail shined in the moonlight. It became known as the Ghost Horse.

Mustangs had short backs, smooth muscles and rounded rumps, and set tails. Their hooves were thick, called a mule hoof. Their legs were fairly short and stocky. The mane and tail of the buffalo horse were long and dark, with another color fringe. A dorsal stripe of hair trailed from the mane to the tail; it had tiger striped foreleg markings. The Blackfeet prized the Spanish Mustang as a dependable buffalo runner and war horse. Their name for the Mustang was "wakiya," in Blackfeet. The Spanish Mustang was one of the finest horses in America, circa 1600.

#17. Hunting Buffalo on Horseback
Len Sodenkamp, Boise Artist

As the Blackfeet attained horses, their whole style of hunting buffalo radically changed. The horse and buffalo were the salvation for the Plains Indian. On horseback, the Indians had mobility to follow the herds easily. Their women could use the horse to pull a travois loaded with teepee hide coverings, necessary camp equipment and infants. The horse and buffalo Indian used the horse to reach the Plains to hunt bison. The horse became the way of life for the Blackfeet. The Plains Blackfeet Indians lived in teepees and hunted buffalo on horseback.

The Indian gentling method of breaking horses to ride was quite different. Four men held the horse's lariat, while a fifth worked with the horse. He grunted in low tones as he walked up to the mustang. He waved a blanket and hissed at the horse, mesmerizing him. Soon, he was able to stroke the head of the animal. The Indian slipped the halter over his head. He still hissed, rubbed its head, neck and flank. A blanket was brushed up against the horse's side, then the other. The horse whisperer threw the blanket over the horse's back. He then mounted and rode the horse. The Blackfeet were excellent horse handlers. Pack horses were broke in for hauling loads using rocks to represent weight they would be carrying.

Lassoes (Lariats) were made from buffalo or elk hides and used primarily with horses. They were normally strips of leather twenty feet long and two fingers wide. Other ropes were made of braided buffalo or horse hair. Indians braided the hair from the mane and tail of horses and the forelock of the buffalo into ropes. Animal hair stuffed dolls, and pillows.

The Blackfeet did not practice selective breeding like the Nez Perce did with their Appaloosa horse, but picked characteristics like color, size and swiftness. The old saying about being born in the saddle tends to describe the Blackfeet Indians, who learned to ride a horse by the time they were five years of age. The Plains Indians rode horses all of their lives.

Horses were very important to the Blackfeet Indians. Horses could be ridden or raced. The advent of the horse revolutionized the Blackfeet life way. Horses were their whole lives. Special horses were used for buffalo horses and others were utilized as horses for war.

In the morning, the young brave's job was to round up the horses and trail them down to the river to drink. In the same way, the young women carried water from the river for cooking and drinking for the lodge and had to gather firewood, too. Horses were a commodity and used in trade. A medicine man might charge three horses as a fee for lifting a spell or praying for a hunt. A brave might give his lover a horse as a gift. If a brave desired the hand in marriage of an Indian girl, he tied up twenty ponies near her lodge as a bride price. Men loved to gamble, for horses.

The Blackfoot had horses and guns in the early 1700's. They built up their military strength and a strong empire. The fierce Blackfoot became mighty in warfare. They were called "the Lords of the Plains" and were a formidable foe.

The Blackfeet warrior had a favorite war-horse with possibly two or three horses in reserve; he had the Spanish Mustang, a buffalo horse, fast and true. If a warrior died, his horse was sacrificed at the grave. Sometimes twenty horses were killed. The belief system was that the warrior needed his horses to ride for hunting and on the war trail in the afterlife.

Indian saddles were of two general types, the pad saddle and the frame saddle. The pad saddle was popular with the Blackfeet. It was made of two leather pieces, sewn together and stuffed with either feathers or grass. The frame saddle of cottonwood was covered with wet rawhide stretched over it that was shrunk to size. The women's saddle was of this type. Their saddles were adorned with saddle blankets and supple folds of buffalo hide. The saddles were attached by a sole cinch of hair or hide. Hunting or warring Blackfeet warriors mostly rode bareback.

The Plains tipi (teepee) came after the horse; it was a large tent, constructed over four lodge poles nearly 20 feet long in a conical-shaped framework, tied at the top. Sinew sewed the buffalo skins together. Covered with eight to twenty buffalo skins, it was anchored at the base with rocks. They were collapsible for travel on a travois. The teepee pit fire for cooking and warmth was in the center; a smoke vent was at the top. Skin mats lay on the floor for comfort with fur blankets used to sleep or recline. The entrance faced toward the rising sun with a circular doorway or v-shaped with skin flaps. It was well insulated. The place of honor was at the rear.

The teepee (wigwam) set up and came down easily. The teepees were collapsed, folded and hauled on two poles, drug behind a horse, called a travois. The horse-travois was larger, able to drag lodge-poles, carry goods, teepee skins, and hides. Infants were hauled this way. With additional poles, a tipi ("teepee") was erected. Blackfeet Indians used four pole lodges.

Teepees and the High Plains way of life and buffalo skins made good coverings. The teepees were painted with bright colors and symbols on the interior consisted of the sky gods, the Sun, Moon and Stars. Animals and bird symbols were also included. Artwork on the outside of a teepee may have shown displays in dozens of illustrations of scenes of animals or war.

#18. Plains Buffalo
Author Photo

Buffalo hunters followed the bison onto the Plains. Their best buffalo horses were used in the hunt. The Blackfeet sent out scouts to determine the location of the buffalo herds. Hunters approached, downwind to not frighten them as the buffalo grazed; the bison herd was fidgety and sensed their presence. The bison's sense of smell exceeded their eyesight. Hunters gave out war whoops and the buffalo stampeded; the chase was on. Braves rode at a gallop alongside the stampeding buffalo. An arrow shot between the bison's ribs penetrated the lung, and dropped the beast.

Buffalo lances were made of saplings about an inch in diameter. They averaged seven to nine feet in length. Crow lances measured twelve feet in length, while Comanche staffs extended to fourteen feet, at times. Buffalo lances were wrapped with the fur of an otter or mink. These were adorned with strips of calico, eagle feathers and beads.

The buffalo lance was a hand-held spear used to thrust and jab or be thrown. A vital spot on the buffalo was behind the shoulder or the last rib. In the same way, the hunter rode alongside the bison, and with a few quick jabs of his lance into the lung brought the animal down. The lance was effective with the Indian, horse and buffalo.

In historic times, the rifle was also used on the bison hunt. A couple of sharp cracks of rifle fire and a buffalo dropped dead as several hunters shot buffalo, much meat was jerked. Traditionally, the buffalo hunt lasted through the fall. The elderly, women and children normally remained behind in Bitterroot Valley, while some braves stayed behind to guard them. The buffalo hunters returned with fresh jerky and buffalo robes for winter.

Horse Blackfeet bison hunters killed enough buffalo to feed their extended family and shared the kill with other families. They guarded the buffalo herds and ran off any intruders. Many hundreds of buffalo were slain annually. The buffalo was one of the largest land creatures hunted by these Indians. The Blackfeet skinned the buffalo and jerked the meat. Pack horses or mules were taken on the expedition to haul the buffalo meat and robes back to camp. The Blackfeet honored the buffalo. It provided them with nearly all of their needs to survive.

In 1871, the U.S. Congress ended the process of making treaties with Indians. They sponsored programs for wholesale slaughter of the buffalo on the Plains in order to force the Indians onto the reservations (1871-1879). Hundreds of Blackfoot people died during this period.

# Chapter Four
## War Path

Tradition of the Montana Blackfeet tells us that they had gotten their horses from the Flathead and Shoshoni Indians. The Blackfeet were known to have sold horses to the Plains tribes, but did not purchase from them. The Comanche, on the other hand, sold horses to the Kiowa and tribes of the Central Plains. The Shoshoni attained their horses from the Comanche Indians, a southern Shoshoni tribe, who stole horses from the Apache Indians in New Mexico. The Arapaho, Bannock, Crow, Kiowa, Nez Perce and Palouse attained horses from the Shoshoni. The Nez Perce and the Palouse tribe had the Appaloosa horse. The name "Appaloosa" came from the Palouse tribe.

The Blackfeet were one of the first tribes to obtain horses and guns. The Indians first called the rifle a Mystery iron, thinking it was magic that fire came out of the end of a stick, like a thunderbolt. Horses were used for war horses and hunting. They literally dominated the Plains on horseback with their military strength. Horse Blackfeet warriors rode out with the intent to capture horses.

Faces were painted for important events. Different patterns stood for war, religious meaning and various festivities. Tattooing was popular for both sexes. Men and women wore tattoos on their faces. The Blackfeet painted their faces, bodies and horses for war and the hunt. Symbol accounts of bravery and war were painted on the war horses. A hand print meant hand to hand combat. The Lords the Plains were a formidable foe.

Stripes on the front legs stood for the amount of coups of the warrior. A fancy hide bonnet was made for the horse, and the bridle was adorned with feathers. The riders wore full Plains regalia and were equipped with a complete array of war shields, guns, and lances. Their bodies were fully painted, giving a masked effect to cause fear into the enemy.

Their warriors performed the Horse Dance, a type of war dance on horseback. Horses were painted red on one side and blue on the other for the Horse Dance. Bridles, saddles and pommels were heavily beaded. Ribbons were tied in the manes and tails. The loved their horses. Their ponies also were painted and adorned with ribbons. Red paint on horses was a favorite of the Blackfeet. Horse-mounted warriors circled and charged in mock battle, gave war whoops and shrill war cries, while firing rifles in the air during their dance. The mock war dance enacted their being at war.

#19. Blackfeet War Party
(Photograph Courtesy of Azusa Publishing, LLC)

The Blackfeet warrior relied on his spirit guide and medicine bundle to lead him in war with the enemy. War Medicine came from his sacred bundle transferred from the Sun, Moon, Stars and Mother Earth. He prayed he would be made invisible when raiding horses. Raids were done at night by small war parties. They were purposefully planned and raided after dark.

The Blackfeet divided the Shoshoni on the Plains and drove them westward into the mountains and onto the Idaho Plateau. These Indians were the Lemhi Shoshoni. An aged 115 year old Sheep-eater woman told of how they were driven into the hills and mountains by the fierce Blackfeet.

This band did not have horses or firearms and used dogs to haul their loads. The need for the dog travois was nearly eliminated by the horse. The Sheepeaters hunted the mountain sheep and goats and lodged among the clouds, high in the mountain crags. Their garments were animal skins. They were called the "Wild Men of the Mountains," by Lewis and Clark, who referred to them as the Broken Moccasin Indians. Later, the Sheepeaters were removed to the reserve and joined the Lemhi Shoshonis.

The aggressive Blackfeet were naturally warring Indians and left their lodges in Montana Country to attack their neighboring enemy camps in what became Idaho Territory. They warred on neighboring tribes on horseback and appeared out of the darkness to run off their horses. The marauders raided unsuspecting Indian camps for horses, plunder, scalps and slaves, counting coup. The braves chose spirited horses and it was great sport to raid for horses. Those camps stole Blackfeet horses in retaliation. The fierce Blackfeet crossed the Rockies to raid for horses from the Cree, Crow, Flathead, Sioux and Shoshoni.

The Blackfeet literally drove the Flathead, Kutenai and Shoshoni from the Plains, out of the Upper Missouri River region, westward onto the Pacific Plateau. The Shoshoni constantly battled the Blackfeet tribe from 1750 to 1805. In 1754, when the Blackfeet Indians were contacted, they had many horses. Their defense was living in large numbers.

The Blackfeet dwelled in large tribal camps (villages) to better defend themselves from attack, but in winter they split up into smaller bands of ten to twenty lodges. The Blackfeet actually dominated the region known as Blackfeet Country. They were hated and feared by smaller bands.

Blackfeet warriors stole many horses by raiding the Shoshoni, Bannock and Flathead camps in the Plateau region. Night raids to steal mustangs came fast and furious. The Blackfeet had a deep-seated hostility toward the Shoshoni Indians, and nearly obliterated the Northern Shoshoni.

Blackfeet attacks on smaller villages greatly reduced their numbers; they seemed to believe that other tribes had trespassed on their territory.

The Flathead Indians hoped to avoid the Blackfeet on their buffalo hunting expedition over the Continental Divide, reaching the prairie east of the Flathead River. Instead, they were ambushed by the Blackfeet, who may have ridden in on the "Warrior Trail." The battle ground was called Bloody Hill. The outcome was not known, but a Flathead brave lived to tell the story.

The Lolo Trail was used by the horse-mounted Nez Perce as a route to access the buffalo plain country. Although the Nez Perce acquired the horse shortly after 1700, they were prevented from hunting the buffalo by heavily armed Blackfeet warriors. The Nez fought back. Lawyer, a Nez Perce Chief, sustained a battle wound from the Blackfeet that pained him for many years.

The boldest Nez Perce hunting parties did not venture far onto the Plains, until after Lewis and Clark came. During the northwest fur trade, the Nez Perce Indians had firearms and were a better match for the Blackfeet on their own terms.

From late summer into autumn, Shoshoni buffalo eaters crossed to the upper Missouri River along the Bannock Trail to hunt buffalo in Montana, invading Blackfeet and Crow Indian territory. The Bannock Trail connected the river plains of central Idaho and the eastern plains of Montana. Mountain Crow dwelled in the Bighorn Valley and the River Crow along the flowing headwaters of the Yellowstone River in Montana. Their biggest threat was the fierce Blackfeet Indian tribe, but the Mountain and River Crow also would give them a good fight, if discovered.

Roving Blackfeet Indians were on the lookout for Shoshoni buffalo hunters crossing along the Bannock Trail in ambush, to attack these tribes for their horses, scalps and spoils that they could steal while counting coup. The Shoshonis kept a constant vigil for them. As the herds of buffalo dwindled, they became more aggressive. The Blackfeet often preyed on Shoshoni hunting parties and raid at any time to take Shoshoni ponies.

The Blackfeet were a big threat to Shoshoni hunting parties that rode to the Upper Missouri and the Plains to hunt bison. Various allies hunted together. The Coeur d'Alene joined the Bannock, Colville, Lower Pend d' Oreille, Spokane and Shoshoni to form huge hunting parties and carefully crossed enemy lands. The Kutenai, Flathead, Kalispel and Nez Perce Indians did the same for their own safety.

The Blackfeet Indians dominated the Plains.    The surrounding neighbors lived in fear of the raiders, who not only raided for horses, but scalps.  Men, women and children were not exempt. Neighboring Shoshoni and other tribes lived in terror of being captured. The only reprieve for a young woman was to be captured for a wife or slave.  Female prisoners were normally treated quite well. Male prisoners were killed and scalped, used to count coup, flogged and held as slaves or were given a reprieve. On rare occasions, slaves were freed. Sometimes a male slave was taken by the chief to the edge of camp, given a horse and provisions and released.

Blackfeet raiders in the Nineteenth Century would attack any Indian camp that was not an ally for horses.  They attacked any enemy as revenge for a skirmish that they lost or to defend their camp or hunting grounds. Their numbers varied from a few into the hundreds.

Blackfeet warriors were largely men; but often women warriors got in the frey of battle.  During their attacks, the Blackfeet would run down and kill fleeing old people, women and children as the enemy, without remorse. Spoils garnered in raids were most likely high spirited horses and captive maidens, for brides, according to Indian custom.

Women were stolen for slaves and struck with coup sticks, sexually attacked or killed.  Sometimes the climate changed and they were spared and protected.  Being taken as a slave was a realistic alternative to being killed by the Blackfeet.  The slaves were given all the rights and privileges of the Blackfeet. Children were adopted or used as slaves.

Men were more likely to be scalped and not captured, but some were captured for slaves, but were often brutally killed.  If an enemy was captured as a slave, he dare not try to fight his captors.  The warriors tried to scalp them and they were in the hands of their captors.  The Blackfeet women and children would beat them with sticks and throw dirt on them.  A male slave was rarely tied and bound, but was watched.

Around the same time of becoming a man, the brave was expected to learn to count coup, a way of reaching manhood.  "Coup," in French meant touch.   To prove his valor, a brave was to rush up to the enemy and touch the warrior like a game; the brave would either run or ride up to the enemy gets in his face and touches him with his hand, a stick or riding quirt to show bravery.   The coup in the eyes of the Plains Indians was a brave act or victory over the enemy.  To enter an enemy camp at night and take horses was another means of counting coup for each horse stolen.  Horses made up wealth.  Killing an enemy with a tomahawk was to exhibit more bravery.

#20. Appaloosa Horse
(Photograph Courtesy of Jumper Horse/Sport

War honors were graded on the basis of the degree of courage displayed in winning them. The capture of a rifle was the highest honor. Killing an enemy with a bow and arrow or rifle at a distance was a high ranking score. The capture of a bow and arrows, ceremonial object, lance, gun, medicine pipe, war bonnet, war-shield or war-shirt counted as a coup of high rank. Capturing a horse or taking a scalp was lower ranked.

Songs were sung on the way home along the war trail, by the scalp hunters. Trophies were displayed on poles and carried by the women in the scalp dance.

The Blackfeet and Crow lodged far from the Oregon Trail and did not become involved in warfare with the United States. Instead, they served as scouts in the Army, although there was some conflict with the fur trappers. The Blackfeet stayed busy hunting buffalo, raided for horses and enjoyed bartering at the fur trade forts.

Montana Territory was Blackfeet country, as well as home to the Mountain and River Crow. The Blackfeet lodged not far from the Crow in Buffalo Country and were possessive of their lands. The Crow Indians were also fierce warriors and the enemies of the Blackfeet, who had grown more militant in time with a strong socio-political structure and strong allies.

The Blackfeet Indians were dominant on the Plains. They were of large stature, muscular and one of the most fierce and warlike tribes of the Amerindians. They dominated the Plains and feared no foe. Militant Blackfeet Indians had been an aggressive tribe since their prehistory. They were a restless breed and naturally predatory. They were constantly at war; they normally repelled their enemies.

The Blackfeet became bloodthirsty warriors in battle and took scalps of their adversaries, counting coup. The Blackfeet Indians practiced scalping their fallen rivals. The warriors often scalped them and did scalp dances over their bodies. Their enemies that they killed in battle were mutilated and dismembered to show power over them. There were two types of scalps: the French scalp, that was the size of a silver dollar, and the full crown scalp, that took all of the hair and scalp. They took scalps of either sex, counting coup.

The Medicine Coup Stick was a long stick with a hook on the end, decorated with otter fur, feathers and paint. The Medicine Coup Stick was also used to count coup on the enemy. A bow, lance or the brave's hand could be used in counting coup, to touch the enemy. Leaders staffs, similar to a coup stick, were decorated with foxtails, hawk or eagle feathers.

#21. Painted Piegan Teepees
(Photograph Courtesy of Azusa Publishing, LLC)

If a warrior struck his opponent, killed him and then scalped him, he counted three coups. A scalp lock was a shared portion of the scalp taken. Human scalps were also displayed as trophies that hung from lodges, war shields and their horses' bridles. Scalps were used as sacrifices to their gods.

The human scalp was stretched over a hoop stick called a Scalp Stick. It was painted black or black and red. The women would carry the scalp stick during the "Scalp Dance." It was believed that the human spirit dwelled in the scalp. The Scalp Dance was a dance performed only by Blackfeet Indian women. They carried scalp sticks during the ceremony while they danced the Scalp Dance. The men danced a victory dance for scalps taken.

The Bannock Indian hunting parties rode to hunt buffalo on the Missouri River along the Bannock Trail. When Blackfeet warriors fought the Bannock Indians, however, the Bannock fought back. They too took scalps, but of the Blackfeet warriors.

Plains Indians were superstitious and would not scalp Negroes or buffalo soldiers. They thought that their scruffy hair too much resembled the fur of the buffalo. They did not always kill their victims. Sometimes they scalped the enemy alive and let them return to their villages in shame. At times, the victor left the scalp on a buffalo chip, as sacrifice to their gods. A Blackfeet warrior might have uttered a short prayer, raising the scalp to the Sun-god.

They first began to acquire horses and found a new life style. Horses meant prosperity. With the horse, they became Plains Indians. The Blackfeet acquired the teepee and travois. They used horses for bride price or a gift for their mother-in-law.

Horses made the hunt and the war trail easier. Raids on horseback were fast, furious and rewarding. Coup was counted with the number of stolen horses and scalps. Wives or slaves could be garnered on horseback. They could plunder and gain a strong bow or lance.

They netted large herds of horses and tribal wealth. The militant Blackfeet were not willing to share the buffalo with other tribes. They attacked the Nez Perce on the Lolo Trail and ambushed the Shoshoni on the Old Bannock Trail as they went to hunt buffalo on the Upper Missouri. They routed and chased any Indians trespassing on their lands.

Horses clearly achieved greater mobility to fight the enemies in warfare. Horse Indians had an advantage to do battle. Horses allowed night raids on enemy camps to take horses. They had the horse for over 170 years. The horse revolutionized the Indians' life way.

#22. Piegan Chief in Full Regalia
(Photograph Courtesy of Azusa Publishing, LLC)

# Chapter Five
## Women Warriors

Occasionally, women, especially widows, became warriors and rode with the men to war. This story was told to the famous archeologist, A.L. Kroeber in Montana by an Atsina (Gros Ventre of the Mountains) Indian woman named Watches All. She looked back at the time that her tribe attacked the Piegan enemy in 1867.

She recalled a gambling game, like poker, between her and a Crow woman where she lost all of her beads in one hand. Her mother punished her and she cried. Watches All joined an Atsina war party because she was mad at her mother. Her mother caught up to them, bringing extra horses for Watches All. They continued on with the war party. The warriors were afoot; the women rode horses. They advanced against the Piegan enemy.

They grew close to the enemy, painted their faces and limbs, danced and sang songs of war. One warrior shaman petitioned his ghost and asked how many Piegan were in the village? The spirit said that there were as many as if they were grass. The spirit said they could kill two people and take some horses; if they killed more, many Gros Ventre would die.

They ignored the warning and killed three men and a woman, instead. The Piegan warriors chased them; they ran for their lives. The Piegan overran them and many were slain. Watches All was captured, but her mother escaped.

The Blackfeet took Watches All back to camp, beat her and stole her clothing. When her mother returned, her husband threatened to kill her unless she rescued her; she returned to the Piegan encampment alone.

Two Piegan warriors claimed the capture of Watches All. She was told to tell which one was her captor. She named No Chief and the other warrior tried to kill her. No Chief took her as his bride and protected her. Another warrior took her mother as his wife. No Chief traded his new bride for two horses, which made Watches All angry. Never-the-less, she did her work and tried to get along with her husband's other wives. She liked her husband and his young son and made him promise not to trade her, since she wanted to return someday to her people.

One year later, Watches All and her mother planned their escape. As the Piegan slept, Watches All slipped out of her lodge and joined her mother. They began to run and continued to run all night. They hid during the daylight and ran all through the night for four nights straight. Once, they

#23. Bannock People
(Photograph Courtesy of Azusa Publishing, LLC)

came close to a sleeping bear. They reached the Missouri River and saw a steamboat. Her mother wanted to board the boat and go to Fort Benton and sell her daughter to the white people. Not choosing to go, Watches All held her mother back and even pulled her knife to threaten her. She pulled away and they made their way toward the river.

The pair saw another boat that had Atsina and Crow Indian passengers. They ran along the river and called to them. The boat slowed to a stop and they boarded. The captain let them off at a saloon and store near a Crow encampment.

Seeing their bruised feet, the Crow women took pity on them. The owner got out some whiskey and gave them some. Soon, Watches All's mother passed out. Then, Sioux Indians killed a man cutting wood for the steamboats. The women inside feared the wild Sioux warriors.

Watches All and her mother caught another boat downstream, with a party of Atsina on board. They saw a buffalo swimming across river and caught it by the horns; they dragged the beast onto the bank and slaughtered it for a big feast! They departed the boat at Milk River and trekked up river until they reached their tribe who was happy to see them again.

*****

Elk Woman (*Ponoka'ki*) was the beautiful wife of Calf Looking (*Onista'miwa*), sub-chief of a Blackfeet band. Calf Looking referred to the calf of the buffalo. They had two children. It was the season of the year when the prickly pear was ripened. Their encampment was south of the Little Bow River about one day's ride on horseback from the prickly pear cactus patch. Elk woman wished to make the journey to pick the prickly pears. Several women in the camp elected to go along and Calf Looking accompanied them. They arrived at the site and Calf Looking was perched upon a foothill of the Rocky Mountains as lookout to oversee the operation. He observed the women as they harvested the prickly pears.

Chief Calf Looking mistook a Shoshoni war party for a small herd of stampeding buffalo. As they came into view, the thundering hoof beats and war whoops of the Shoshoni warriors could be heard. Calf Looking signaled the women and descended the hill as the Shoshoni rode nearer at a full gallop. The women dropped the pears, mounted their horses and rode off. The Shoshoni on fine horses overtook them. One by one they caught the stragglers on tired horses and killed them by tomahawk or arrows.

#24. Crow Indian & Medicine Coup Stick
(Photograph Courtesy of Azusa Publishing, LLC)

Elk Woman shouted at her husband to come back and save her. He reined up, swung his horse around and rode back to her. He pulled her up behind him onto his horse and as she wrapped her arms tightly around his waist, Calf Looking spurred his mustang. They had a comfortable lead at a gallop, but his buffalo horse began to tire from them riding double. With the Shoshoni fast approaching, Calf Looking told his wife that he had an idea, and told her to dismount and explained that she was young and pretty and would not be killed. His plan was to come back after her with a large war party and save her. She sobbed and begged that they could die together, but he stuck to his plan and pushed her off his horse.

Calf Looking rode off at a full gallop, unseen by the Shoshoni, in hot pursuit. He arrived at the camp and broadcast what had occurred. He cut his hair, painted his face black, and wore rags, in mourning for Elk Woman, his wife. Family and friends went into mourning, too. They all smoked the pipe together and agreed on the intended rescue. The chief told them that when they returned to camp, a war party would be formed to follow the Shoshoni.

Soon, Chief Calf Looking organized a search party of his three brothers and his three brothers-in-law and rode back along the war trail. They followed the path to the prickly pears. The party found the bodies of the women slain by the Shoshoni warriors, but not that of Elk Woman.

They followed the tracks of the Shoshoni war party south across the grassy prairie. As they reached a large river, the party could see smoke ascending from the lodges of the Shoshoni encampment. The Blackfeet took cover in some trees near a hill at the base of the Rockies across the river.

Calf Looking volunteered to swim across the river in search of his wife, Elk Woman, just before twilight. He swam the river and crawled up on the bank, surveying the situation. He wrapped a blanket around him, pulled it over his face and began looking for Elk Woman. Methodical, he went from teepee to teepee in search of her. Finally, he came to a large teepee in the center and peered in through a slot in the flap of the door.

On the floor sat Elk Woman with the Shoshoni Chief's baby on her breast. Elk Woman related the story of a warrior claiming her to Calf Looking. Another warrior had challenged him for her. In the end, they took Elk Woman and gifted her to the Shoshoni Chief. She was so young and beautiful that the Chief took her for a wife, instead of making her a slave. Calf Looking slipped away, determined to catch her alone, away from the lodge. As the women walked the path to go draw water from the river, he hid and watched. It was here that the young braves dared to meet their lovers.

71

#25. Crow Hardship, Curtis
(Photograph Courtesy of Azusa Publishing, LLC)

Later in the day, Elk Woman walked slowly toward the river carrying her vessel. He stepped out and spoke with her. The young chief explained to her that her brother's position was across river in the trees, and that they had come with him to rescue her and urged Elk Woman to join them. She told him that the Shoshoni had given her many gifts and she wanted to go back and get them. She said at nightfall she would steal a horse and join them.

Instead, as she walked back, Elk Woman picked up some charcoal and put it in her mouth. The black substance drooled from her mouth, as she fell on the ground, feigning the contortions of a fit. She was lying there moaning, when the Chief and the others found her. He carried her into the lodge and called for the medicine man.

The Indians crowded around her. She sat up, feeling better and began to speak in sign language. "The Sun god," she said, "struck her down and Elk Woman was given a spirit." The crowd in the lodge stirred. Elk Woman told them that the Sun spirit told her that seven enemies hid across the river in a grove of trees. "One warrior, my little brother," she said, "had long glossy hair" She said not to kill the strong chief, who was to be sacrificed.

The Shoshoni ambushed their enemies, hidden in the grove of trees. They attacked, killing all but the Chief. The long, black, silky hair made a fine scalp to present to their Chief.

They bound Calf Looking and moved him into the Chief's lodge. Elk Woman taunted him and offered the young Chief food. He told her that she was needed by their children, but instead she had half of her family killed. "You are heartless," he told her.

The Shoshoni asked in sign language what he had told her. She signed that he said to heap coals on his chest and he would not cry out. So the Chief ordered coals brought in to torture him. "You are pitiless and enjoy my suffering," he sneered. Again, she signed to the Shoshoni, telling them that he dared the Chief to have scalding hot water poured on his head.

The Chief had hot water poured onto his head until chunks of his hair fell out, burning him badly. Again, Elk Woman signed to them that the Sun spirit wanted his sacrifice. The Chief agreed and had Calf Looking bound tightly to a tree. They broke camp and moved on to another location.

An old woman, who begged for food in the Shoshoni encampment, took pity on Calf Looking. She adopted him as her son and cut him loose. She agreed to join her people and leave a green stake in the ground every time they moved camp, pointing the direction of their travel. She fed him and gave the chief a pair of moccasins to wear; they agreed to meet in camp.

#26.. Piegan Encampment
(Photograph Courtesy of Azusa Publishing, LLC

Calf Looking returned to the Blackfeet encampment and explained to her parents and others what Elk Woman had done, calling her a she-devil. Her mother sharpened her axe, ready to kill Elk Woman. There was murmuring in the camp of Elk Woman's betrayal.

The warriors caught their horses and gathered their finest weapons for war. Calf Looking was treated by the medicine man for his wounds. Soon, they were on the warpath. When the war party reached the river, vultures circled overhead. They had left the dead lying there.

They found the Shoshoni camp abandoned. The war party picked up the sign of tracks and found old mother's green stake pointed west. Some argued that she could not be trusted, but Calf Looking put their fears aside. They continued west over the prairie, until the scouts returned to say they had located the Shoshoni camp, just past the second ridge, where there was cover. Between the first and second ridge lay a gully, where they hid.

It was time for revenge; the war party sneaked into the Shoshoni camp. Calf Looking located the old woman's teepee and tried to quiet her big black dog; she calmed the dog. He stepped into her lodge and kissed her. Calf Looking asked about his wife. She was highly esteemed now, believed to have strong powers, the old woman told him and pointed toward the central teepee. Calf Looking led her back to the coulee.

At daybreak, the Blackfeet swept in from the ridge as the warriors rode in to ambush the Shoshoni, taking them completely by surprise. With bow and arrows, tomahawks and lances, the warriors stormed the camp. Wolf Leading Along, Elk Woman's brother, led the attack. The raid was a success and Calf Looking said that he wanted Elk Woman taken alive.

The warriors fought the braves, giving women and children a chance to flee to safety; Wolf Leading Along headed for the Chief's teepee and Elk Woman. The Chief was slain. The woman in the lodge cried out, "Don't hurt me, I am Blackfeet. Are any of my people with you?"

Elk Woman was seized and bound, until the siege ended. Her mother, tomahawk in hand, tried to end it all, but was restrained. She wanted vengeance for her sons and threatened the Snake woman's life. Instead, Elk Woman was brought before Calf Looking, and the council decided her fate. She spat on Calf Looking and called him a coward, saying that she had her revenge. The council voted and decided that Elk Woman must die for her evil deeds. It was unanimous. Elk Woman was put to death. They scalped the Chief and did the scalp dance.

#27. Shoshoni-Bannock Warriors
(Photograph Courtesy of Azusa Publishing, LLC

The Northern Plains Piegan believed that their gods came to them in dreams. Lance Woman was a beautiful eighteen year old Piegan Indian maiden. She had a dream that Morning Star came to her. He claimed her as his own and said that she must become a woman warrior. Morning Star told Lance Woman that he had long watched her and she was his. He told her not to marry without his consent. Morning Star told her to go on the war trail and take many horses.

Lance Woman had long loved Young Bull; he was proud of her dream and experience. Young Bull said that although he could not marry her, he would be with her on the war trail.

Lance Woman prepared for war and painted the symbol of the Morning Star on her forehead. The war party consisted of ten warriors. Young Bull and her brother, Red Wolf, were among them. A white man, who married a Piegan woman, rode long and far. Pine, a Tewa Indian who had traded with Kit Carson in Taos, was their guide. He led them far to the south.

They traveled for 40 days and reached a valley with adobe buildings, where the Indians served hot food that burned Piegan throats. The women asked Lance Woman to dwell there.

Warriors in her party noticed some Pawnees loitering in the area and warned Lance Woman. The Pawnees wanted her for a sacrifice. Lance Woman was sure that she was safe, but the Pawnee Indians kidnapped her and rode northward toward their homeland. The Piegan heard of her capture and set out to pursue and rescue her. She had no idea of her plight, but she did question why her rape had not occurred.

Following their tracks, the Piegan reached the Pawnee village in twelve moons. Tewa and the white men entered the village and said that they were traders and learned the Pawnee sacrificial ceremony had begun.

On the third day of the festivities, the Pawnee built a scaffold. When the Morning Star appeared in the sky just before dawn, men would take Lance Woman's clothes and tie her to the scaffold, before torching her, setting the scaffold ablaze. One captor would shoot her with a sacred arrow and a shaman would cut her chest open and smear her blood on his face; she would be shot with many arrows and be cut down, left for the coyotes.

The previous evening, Piegan captured some Pawnee horses, counting coup. Fresh horses were to be used to replace their spent horses. They planned the rescue at daybreak. Some Pawnees hated the idea and helped Tewa and the white man gets Red Wolf and Young Bull into the village.

At daybreak, the Pawnee stripped Lance Woman of her clothing and secured her to the structure. She lay there in fear, knowing their plan. She looked to her sun deity to free her from the Wolf people. At that moment, the Piegan attacked. The white man cut her bindings and Young Bull carried her to his horse and they rode out of the village. The Piegan took the fresh mounts and fled. A Pawnee arrow killed a Piegan warrior.

Lance Woman was silent for many days, as they rode northwest toward Blackfeet Country. At last, she made her feelings known and announced that she no longer wanted to be a warrior woman. Lance Woman said that she wanted to be a real woman and have what women have; I want my own lodge, now because of my dream, I cannot achieve it.

But, the war chief convinced her that the rescue was Morning Star telling her that she should marry and give up the war path. Now, she and Young Bull could marry and take a lodge.

^^◇^^

The most beautiful woman of all the Blackfeet people was Otter Woman, who was promised to Black Elk. She awaited her lover's return from a raid on the Crow and would move into a new lodge her mother built. There were over 40 warriors in the war party, but Black Elk who had died after killing five warriors in hand-to-hand combat. He was the only one slain. Black Elk' mother and Otter Woman fasted, and wailed in mourning.

After a proper period of mourning, warriors began to appear at the lodge of Eagle Plume, Otter's father, with horses for a bride price. Eagle Plume made a public announcement that Otter Woman would never marry. Otter Woman's parents and Black Elk's mother talked her into marrying Talks-with-the-Buffalo; though he was old enough to be her father. Once, he had saved Eagle Plume's life. He already had two wives and many children.

A warrior named Handsome Man came to the village. Pretty women fell at his feet. Otter Woman sat with *Otahki*, one of Talks-with-the-Buffalo's other wives, while Handsome Man danced. Otter Woman had loaned Otahki a bone-sewing awl. She wanted to ask for it back, but instead asked her to give back Handsome Man; it was a slip of the tongue.

Otahki immediately told their husband. Otter Woman told him that she was a faithful wife and that Handsome Man meant nothing to her. She repeated herself and maintained that it was a mistake and that she was faithful to him. He scowled, shrugged and strolled away.

When Handsome Man heard the story, he swelled with pride. She turned him down when he wanted to meet her at dusk. The next day,

78

Otter Woman and Otahki were going to the river for water. Otahki turned back to get another container. At that time, Handsome Man appeared from the brush and tried to molest Otter Woman. She called him dog-face, bit him and tried to draw her knife, as he grabbed her. She fell backwards; he on top of her. He tried to coax her to make love to him. She fought him off, as Otahki returned, shouting at them.

The following day, Talks-with-the-Buffalo invited his friends and relatives into his lodge to discuss what to do with Otter Woman. Otter Woman maintained her innocence. The gods will not let them punish me since I am innocent. Her parents begged her to leave the old man. Leaving the lodge of my husband would indicate that I was guilty.

Otahki said that she was guilty. Otter Woman said that she was only fighting him off when Otahki came; Talks-with-the-Buffalo remembered what Otter Woman said about Handsome Man and did not believe her. Finally, Bear Head came forward and confessed that he had seen Handsome Man and Otahki in the bushes. Otahki pulled the blanket over her head in shame. Her husband then demanded she tell the truth or he would cut out her tongue. He took his knife and disfigured her face. The adulteress was forced to beg in the streets all of her life. Otter Woman was honored, but nearly became an outcast for one slip of the tongue.

~◇~

Brown Weasel Woman loved to go hunting with her father as a child. To the objection of his wives, he made her a bow and arrows and taught her to shoot accurately. Much later on a hunting trip, an enemy war party attacked them. They shot the horse out from under her father. Brown Weasel Woman spurred her horse and rode directly into the enemy ranks and rescued her father. Warriors, who witnessed it, praised Brown Weasel Woman for her actions. They told the story over and over again. At the same time, the women of the village gossiped about her.

Meanwhile, Brown Weasel Woman's mother became seriously ill. Being the oldest, she took over her mother's duties in the lodge. She cooked and tanned hides and taught her siblings to help. Her mother watched from her bed. The women quit gossiping.

Brown Weasel Woman yearned to go to war again. She let her brothers and sisters do the work at home. The young men did not interest her. Her father was killed on a raid against the Crow Indians. It was not long before her mother passed, too. Older sister found a widow to take care of her siblings. She took down her father's rifle and prepared to go to war.

The mourning period was over and Brown Weasel Woman was ready for the war path.

Piegan warriors formed a war party to raid the Crows' camp for horses and asked Brown Weasel Woman to join them on the raid. They garnered many horses; Brown Weasel Woman, alone, took eleven. On the trip home, she stood guard, while the other warriors rested. Two Crow warriors, determined to retrieve their horses, caught up to the Piegan war party. Brown Weasel woman shot and killed one warrior and grabbed the other's rifle. He fired but she dodged the bullet. Other warriors seized him.

They scalped the fallen warrior and presented her with the scalp. She did not want the scalp, but accepted it as revenge for her father's death. Some looked down on her for her actions. One shaman told her to go and fast, to seek her vision. Brown Weasel woman was gone four days alone in the wild. She fasted and prayed; at last she saw her vision. From then on, no one doubted her and accepted her as a woman warrior.

Woman warriors had followed the war path in the past, but only with their husbands. Brown Weasel Woman was the first to go on the war path, solo. After a successful raid on the Kalispel Indians, the warriors asked her to recant her brave deeds. She recanted her feats and received praise. The head chief prayed before making a speech, which gave her a new name, Running Eagle, a highly regarded name of other famous warriors.

Brown Weasel Woman was invited to join the Brave's Society. Her feats of bravery in taking horses and killing enemy warriors became legend among the Blackfeet people. Many warriors courted her, but she never aspired to marry. She led war parties. Flathead Indians killed some Piegan warriors hunting buffalo; and in retaliation, she led a Blackfeet war party. Fighting with the Flatheads, a warrior attacked her with a war club. She killed him as another warrior closed in from behind and killed her with his tomahawk. Running Eagle died on the war trail. One of her warriors killed her attacker, as the battle ended. Her people mourned her death and proclaimed her to be the greatest woman warrior of the Blackfeet Nation.

∧∧◇∧∧

The Horse Medicine cult was initiated by a Blackfeet Indian named Wolf Calf, also called Pemmican Maker. Wolf Calf was the cult leader. The cult ceremony was the horse dance and the exchange of the most secret horse medicine (*pono-ka-mita saa'm*). A Blackfeet woman named Ghost Woman was the only female horse handler to claim to have horse medicinal powers. Horse raisers were believed to possess secret powers.

# Chapter Six
## Ghost Stories
## & Lodge Tales

When a person died, the usual method of burial was to wrap the body in a robe or blanket and place the body on a scaffold or poles elevated in the air on a platform on a hill or in a tree. Personal possessions were placed near the body: bow and arrows, other weapons, pipe, war garb and medicines.

In historic times, a person who died might be left in his lodge, his bed was made and the flaps sewn shut. This was referred to as a death lodge. Often, his horses were shot and placed near the warrior. If a chief died, the band might move and leave him in his lodge. Graves in historic times were underground. There was a period of mourning where the relatives cut their hair short. Women gashed their legs and arms with a knife and wore plain clothing and no jewelry. Wailing was common for the women at the time.

The Blackfoot were very superstitious and feared ghosts. The Indians told dozens of legendary ghost stories and loved to hear them. They believed in ghosts, and ghosts played a big part in their lives. Ghosts were part of their tradition and were associated with the dead, whose spirits were believed to travel to a place called the Sand Hills in Canada, their nirvana or heaven. The spirit world was parallel to life on earth. The dead were invincible to the living. People were afraid to travel alone at night and the Blackfoot Indians embraced haunting as reality.

Their children were taught early to fear ghosts and be brave. Their parents also taught them to cope with phantoms. If a young child was sick, a medicine man might be called in to remove the evil spirits. To speak a dead person's name was taboo. A synonym like "the person we loved" was substituted, instead. Use of the word, "ghost" (*sta-au*) was also taboo.

The Indian people were sometimes attached to spirits. They believed that ghosts might dwell near their loved ones for protection and romanced them. A bone from a family member was kept occasionally to encourage their apparition to dwell there.

*****

There was a man who dearly loved his wife. It was not long until they had a baby boy. In time, the mother grew ill and did not recover. After an extended illness, she became worse. The shaman prayed over her, but she lapsed and died.

#28. Enemy Mountain Crow
(Photograph Courtesy of Azusa Publishing, LLC

The husband took no new wife. He mourned a long time after her death. He packed the boy around and wept as he walked in the hills. He was beside himself. After a time he told his son that he would have to go live with grandmother while he searched for his mother. He promised to bring the boy's mother home with him. He took the child to his grandmother's lodge and left him with her. The young man left the lodge not knowing what to do next, but he left camp and headed for the Sand Hills. Four nights later he had a dream. He dreamed that he entered a small lodge and saw an old woman. She asked, "Why did you come?"

He answered her, "I mourn day and night for my wife, who died some time ago. I search for her. My little son also mourns."

"I saw her," said the woman "she passed this way" but said that she could not help him. He was to go to a butte in the distance, where an old woman would help him on his journey.

"Beyond the butte, near her lodge, you will discover the encampment of the ghosts." The following day, he left early. Reaching the butte, he found no lodge. The man lay down and slept; again he dreamed. He saw a small lodge and walked in to see an old woman.

She spoke to him, "My son, you are not happy. I know why you come this way. You seek your wife who lives in the land of the ghosts. You may not get her back, but I will give you powers. Take my advice and you might succeed." The old woman spoke words of wisdom to him and gave him her medicine. She gave him instructions to help him on his journey.

She went to the ghost camp and planned to bring back some of his relations. If she returned with them, the man was to close his eyes. If you open your eyes and look around, you will die and will never return.

He was instructed that when he passed a big lodge and they asked him, "Where are you going and who told you to come here?" He was to answer, "My grandmother, who is standing just outside here with me told me to come." "They will try and scare you. "You will hear strange noises and see awful things, but do not be afraid," she said.

He passed by a big lodge and a man came out and asked him where he was going. The young man answered, "I seek my dead wife. I mourn for her day and night and cannot rest. My small son cries for her. People of the village have offered other wives, but for naught. I want only the one that I seek." The ghost said, "This is a frightful place; there has never been a mortal here." The ghost asked the man to come into his lodge and he entered. The ghost chief said to him, "After four days, you will see your

#29.  Blackfeet Burial Pyre
(Photograph Courtesy of Azusa Publishing, LLC

wife; but beware, you may never leave alive." The apparition left the lodge and called to the man's father-in-law, "Come to the feast," like the man had died and come as a ghost to the ghost camp.

When the ghosts arrived, they refused to go in because a mortal was within; they could smell a human being. The ghost chief burned sweet pine on a fire. It masked the smell and the ghosts entered. The chief ghost said, "Pity this son-in-law; he seeks his wife. He has come far and is bold. The young man has a tender heart and no mother. He and his son mourn." The spirits told the man that he would be there four nights. At that time we will present you with a medicine pipe, a worm pipe and you may join your wife and return home.

On the third night, the chief of ghosts called all of the ghosts and his wife came. One ghost beat a drum and another carried the worm pipe and gave it to him. The ghost chief told him about the journey home and said his wife should carry the pipe. He was to keep his eyes closed and relatives would accompany them part of the way. His wife was now a person.

"You will open your eyes on the fourth day and see your wife alive. His father-in-law instructed him to have relatives build a sweat lodge. Go and wash thoroughly in the lodge for purity. If you fail, you will die." Ghosts can only be removed by a thorough sweat bath.

He was told never to beat his wife, strike her with a knife blade, or hit her with fire; you strike her she will vanish and return to the ghost camp.

On the fourth day he opened his eyes and the ghosts disappeared and he stood before the old woman's lodge. She said, "Give back my medicine." Nearing the camp, he had the sweat lodge prepared and they bathed in it. He and his wife burned sweet pine, fanned the smoke in and purified their clothing and the Worm Pipe, also.

The man relayed to them how he retrieved his wife and received the Worm Pipe. The pipe was to belong to the Piegan band, known as the Worm People.

In the evening, he asked his wife to do a task for him. She was slow and he lost patience with her and picked up a firebrand and raised it, as if to hit her. She slowly faded and then vanished, never to be seen again.

*****

Long ago, four Blackfoot was at war with the Cree Indians. The four journeyed a great distance, when their horses gave out and they started for home. As they passed through the Sand Hills, there were travois trails in the sand where people had traveled.

One of them suggested, "Let us follow their trail until we overtake them. They followed the tracks for a long ways. Finally, a Blackfoot warrior, a man of great power named *Ekuskini* spoke, "Why continue? It is nothing."

The others replied, "Not so, these are our people." It was becoming twilight, when they found a stone maul and the travois. "I know these things. They belonged to my mother," one of them said, "They were buried with her; this is odd." It grew dark and they made camp.

Early the next morning, they could hear people talking. A young man was giving war whoops and a woman chopped wood. A man called friends to his lodge for a feast and a smoke.

A variety of sounds emerged from the camp. The four looked, but could see nothing. In fear, they covered their heads with buffalo robes.

Then they took heart and began to explore the area. They looked around, but discovered nothing. Someone spoke, "Look there, and see that *pis'kun* (v-shaped corral)? Let us go take a look at it." As they walked toward it, one of them picked up an arrow. The pis'kun disappeared.

One spoke and said, "There is my father chasing a buffalo. Let us go to him." They saw a man on a white horse in pursuit of a running buffalo. He drew his bow and shot an arrow into its lung, killing the bison. He began to butcher it, and rolled the animal on its back. As the party continued toward him, he mounted his horse and rode off. When they reached the skinning site, there was nothing but a dead mouse and beside it was a buffalo chip with a red arrow on it. One of them said, "That arrow is my father's." He picked it up and the arrow became a blade of grass. He laid it down and immediately it became an arrow again.

*****

A Blackfoot woman died and her husband loved her so much that he left his people and ventured to the land of the dead. The widower journeyed four days and nights to get to the Sand Hills. He reached a village of the dead, and a shadow of a lad appeared. He was just shadow and voice. The man spoke to the apparition and said he was searching for his wife.

The ghost chief took him to a lone tipi and he entered. As he entered the lodge, a voice told him to be seated. The ghost picked up a pipe, filled it and began to smoke. Little by little, the hand and arm of the ghost started to appear. The ghost smoked and handed the pipe to another shadow, which began to appear. They smoked until the pipe was empty and refilled.

"My son," said the ghost chief, "what are you looking for? Why have you journeyed to this place?" The man answered, "I have come to find my wife." "You can sleep here, tonight. Tomorrow, we can look for your wife."

The following day, the chief spoke of four ghost villages in the Sand Hills. The Ghost Chief sent an apparition to the village to tell the women to pass by the live man. One by one they passed by him, but none was his wife. The Chief sent messengers to the second and third village saying that the women there should pass by him, but none was his woman.

The ghost chief told the man that only one village remained and those women passed in front of the Blackfoot man. They came in groups of three and four. As three women came by him, he exclaimed, "There she is." His wife smiled and moved forward to kiss him. "No," said the ghost, "don't touch him." The ghost chief told the man to enter his lodge; he took down the pipe and vowed to teach him the songs and ceremonies of the dead. He invited his shadow friends into the lodge. The chief lifted the man to show how apparitions become visible.

The ghost chief then gave him the pipe to return to his people; the ghost medicine pipe was wrapped in owl skin, decorated with beaver claws and seven eagle feathers. With it was a crow feather fan, a rawhide container and a wooden bowl. He then invited the live man's wife to his lodge. The pipe was purified by the smoke of the sweet pine. As she arose, the chief placed the pipe bundle on her back and said she could return to the land of the living. He instructed the man to not look back, nor look at his wife the whole time. He was to face the west at all times. She was to walk behind him and place the bundle on a tripod at night and sleep beside it.

The man obeyed and walked out of the Sand Hills, followed by his wife. They proceeded west. He did not look back. On the fourth day they reached a hill above their camp. A messenger took a message to his father to set up four sweat lodges in a row, east to west, with the doors facing east, and the messenger did. When the lodges were ready, the man walked down the hill and his wife followed, carrying the pipe bundle. It was placed on the first lodge and they entered.

The ghost medicine pipe bundle was owned by several owners. The second owner was the Blackfoot, Bull Shakes His Head. When a transfer was made, the first owner instructed the people to take an item from the new owner's lodge. The new owner's lodge was stripped. Then, their instruction was to replace each item with a new one. This was a new start for the new bundle owner and the Blackfoot tribe thanks to the generous ghost.

Ghost ceremonies were performed in the traditional Ghost Dance and the Ghost Medicine Pipe Bundle. Sacred bundles were the object of prayers and medicine for the tribe. Bundles were carefully guarded.

*****

This is the story of the Blackfoot Ghost Dance. A young man camped with his wife and young son. The young mother grew ill and died. The brave had no way to feed the baby. Overcome with grief, he left the boy beside his mother's body and sewed the tent flaps shut.

The brave rode away and continued to ride all day. He reached a lodge near a stream that seemed empty. A voice called for him to enter. Hearing the sound of drums and singing, he went in. A fire was burning in the center and there were human bones strewn around. Indian ghosts inside sat cross-legged smoking a pipe. When it was passed around four times, their earthly forms began to appear. The apparitions sang, danced and recanted their war experiences. The brave was sad and had not joined in.

The young man told them how he had to leave his wife and young son behind in the death lodge. The ghost chief asked him if he would invite the ghosts to his lodge. The ghost chief asked him if there was a woman to prepare the lodge. He replied that there was not. He asked him four times before the man agreed. They all returned to the death lodge and sat and smoked the pipe until daybreak and disappeared. The next night the spirits returned. The fourth night his wife sat up and began to prepare a meal.

The ghost chief asked the brave to learn the dance that they had done the four nights and to perform it. The ghost chief instructed the man to do the "Night People's Dance" and take it to the Blackfoot people for their well being. That is how the dance began. The dance was performed after prayer and purification ceremonies. They sang the ghost song in the kneeling position with their fists clenched, then moved and swayed to the music and passed the ghost pipe and said prayers saying they would fear the ghosts.

The Blackfoot people believed that in the Sand Hills, the dead lived in lodges, hunted with horses, exactly like earth. Blackfoot Indians traveling through the Sand Hills swore that they heard noises and saw the deserted camp circles left by the dead. The Sand Hills was a desolate land south of the Saskatchewan River. They believed that some dwelled in the Sand Hills near their bodies. The Blackfoot feared the scalped dead the most. They believed that an enemy who had died in battle would send invisible arrows into persons, causing sickness and death or insanity. Many people that traveled at night hurried to avoid confronting ghosts.

# Lodge Stories

A Blackfoot storyteller, Brings-Down-the-Sun, told the legendary story of Star Boy, also known as *Poia* (Scarface), who was born in the sky and came to earth as Star Boy and lived in poverty among them. Through bravery, he reached the home of the sun, and his scar was healed.

The Sun-god sent Star Boy back to earth to instruct the Blackfoot people in sun worship. After initiating the Sun Dance ceremony, he returned to his sun home, becoming a Morning Star, as a god. Morning Star related sacred stories about constellations.

In Blackfoot folklore, a benevolent creator of the world was a cultural hero called Old Man (*Napi*). His wife was Old Woman (*Kipitaki*). The following is a narrative of the creation.

In the beginning, water covered the earth. One could see nothing but water over the surface. Something floated on the water. It was a raft, and on it were Old Man and the animals. Old Man wanted to create land, so he instructed Beaver to dive down deep to find the bottom and bring up mud. He stayed down a long time, but could not reach the bottom. So he sent down the Loon to find bottom. The Loon tried as hard as it could, but could not reach bottom. Finally Old Man sent down Otter to find the bottom. Otter was gone a very long time and nearly drowned. He was pulled onto the raft; Otter gasped for air. He had mud on his paws.

Old Man dried the mud and scattered it on the water and formed land. He made the rivers and falls; he formed mountains and the prairie. Napi formed the timber, trees and bushes. He made the Sweet Grass Hills and caused the berries and wild vegetables to grow. Old Man made a place for bull berries, camas, service berries and wild turnips to grow.

Napi made the mountain sheep and led it by the horns up in the hills into the mountain crags. Old man said, "This is where you belong." He made the antelope in the mountains. It tried to run, but stumbled and fell. He took it to the prairie and said, "Now you can run free."

One day, Old Man made up his mind to create a woman and a child, so he took clay and molded them into human shape. "You shall be people," he said. He covered them with his robe and came back to check on them for four days. The fourth day he said, "Stand and walk," and they did. They walked down to the river with their creator; he told them his name.

The woman asked him, "Will we live forever and will there be no end to us?" Napi answered, "I have not thought of it. We will throw a buffalo chip into the water and if it floats, we shall live always; if it sinks, there will be an end to them" He threw the buffalo chip into the water and it floated. The woman said, "No, I will throw a stone into the water." The woman threw the stone and it sank." "You have chosen well," said Napi "there will be an end to them." Many nights later, the child died. She cried and cried. She told Napi, "Let us change this rule.

"No," Napi said, "What we have said cannot be changed. The child is dead. People will have to die." The first people had hands like a bear, with claws. They were naked and poor and did not know how to survive. Napi showed them how to dig roots, pick berries and peel the bark from trees to eat. Napi explained how to cook and eat beaver, rabbits and squirrels.

Napi took notice that the buffalo used their horns to gore people and eat them. He found his children on the ground partly eaten. Napi felt bad and went to the people who were still alive. He said, "Something is wrong." I have not made people right. From now on, people will eat the buffalo." He asked, "How is it that the animals are killing you and you do nothing?" "What can we do?" they asked, "They kill us; we have no way to kill them."

Old Man said, "That is not hard. I will show you how to kill these animals." He took a service berry limb, peeled back the bark and made a bow and tied a string on it and took a limb and tied four feathers on it and shot it, but it shot poorly. So, he tied three feathers to the shaft and it shot straight. Old Man Napi broke chips of black flint for arrow points and them not to run when the animals chased, but to shoot them with the bow.

They walked up on a hill and the buffalo said, "There is some food," and rushed towards them. The people stood their ground and instead, shot the buffalo. As arrows hit the buffalo, he said, "My friends, a great fly is biting me." The people killed the buffalo and took chips of the black stone and make knives and cut up the buffalo. Napi said, "It is not healthy to eat buffalo meat raw. He built a fire and showed them how to cook the meat.

Old Man created more human beings and more buffalo at Porcupine Mountains. He breathed life into them. They asked him what they should eat. Napi said, pointing to the buffalo, "There is your food." He took them to a cliff and showed them how to heap up piles of stones to make rows on the cliff, where the buffalo would run and fall over the edge. Below, he built a v-shaped corral to catch them as they fell. Napi called to the buffalo and they ran over the cliff into the corral they had built. He told them to take the sharp knives and cut up the flesh. Some of the buffalo still lived, so he told them how to make stone hammers with handles and smash in their skulls.

90

In later times, Old Man marked the land for the five tribes: the Blackfoot, Blood, Piegan, Gros Ventre and Sarcee. He said to those tribes, "When people come to cross this medicine line bordering your land, take your bows and arrows, lances and war clubs and go on the war trail. Keep them out; if they get a foothold here, trouble will follow."

A tale of Blackfoot mythology is the Buffalo Dance. When buffalo first came to the land, they were not friendly to the people. When hunters tried to coax them over cliffs for the good of the village, they were reluctant to offer themselves up. They did not relish being turned into robes and dried jerky for their rations, nor for their horns to be made into spoons and glue.

"We did not like our sinew being used in sewing and our coats made into their robes." "No, no", they said, "we won't fall into your traps, and we won't fall for any of your tricks." When the hunters guided them toward the cliffs, the wise buffalo turned at the last minute. With the buffalo not cooperating, the village people were hungry, cold and ragged in winter.

Hunter's daughter was proud of her father's skill with his bow. In summer, he brought the best hides to work; she would fashion the deerskins into the most supple, white garments. Her dresses were as soft as a snow goose's down. She made fine garb for her father to wear. The moccasins she crafted for the children and grandmothers in the village were fine gifts.

Snow was coming with the howling winds and deer in the willow breaks. The maiden viewed the reluctance of the stubborn buffalo families that had become a very serious problem. The hunter's daughter decided to try and remedy the situation. The maiden descended to the very base of the cliff and began to sing her song, in a low, soft voice.

"Buffalo family, visit me; come down and feed my guests for a fine wedding feast." She promised that she would join them and become the bride of their very strongest warrior. She paused and listened and thought that she heard the thunder of many hooves in the distance. Again she sang, "Buffalo family, visit me. Feed us in the wedding feast. I can be a bride."

The thundering sound grew louder; the buffalo family began falling at her feet. One very large buffalo fell on top of other buffalo and walked across their backs. The bull announced that he was here to claim his bride. "I am afraid to join you," the maiden said. "You must, my people gave themselves for the feast," the bull said.

I must tell all of my relatives the good news, she exclaimed. Large buffalo said, "No." He picked her up and carried her off between his horns, over to the buffalo's village. The next day, the whole village started looking

91

for the hunter's daughter. They found the heap of buffalos below the cliff. Her father, being a good tracker and hunter, found her tracks in the dirt.

"The buffalo took her. I will follow their tracks," he said. Hunter walked for hours. He grew tired and sat down by a buffalo wallow. Magpie came by and sat down beside him. Hunter spoke to Magpie. "My daughter was taken from me by a buffalo. Can you find them?" Magpie said that he had seen them. "They are resting on the other side of the hill."

"Magpie, will you go tell my daughter I am just this side of the hill?" asked Hunter. Magpie flew over the hill to the grassy meadow, where Buffalo lay asleep with other buffalo. The Magpie hopped over to Hunter's daughter who was sewing porcupine quills on moccasins. "Your father is just over the hill waiting for you," said Magpie to the Hunter's daughter.

"This is dangerous," she said to Magpie. "The buffalo could hurt my father. "Please just ask Hunter to wait for me," she said, "I will take leave of the buffalo and meet him." Her husband, Buffalo, took off his horn and asked her to go fill it with water from the wallow. She carried the horn over the hill. Hunter crouched down and gestured her to come with him.

"No," she replied. "The buffalo are angry with us for killing buffalo people, they will chase us and trample us in the dirt," she said, and took the water to her husband; he took a drink, snorted and gave a loud bellow. They stood up, raised their tails in the air did the Buffalo Dance.

While dancing, they trampled Hunter. His daughter sat down by the wallow and sobbed. Her husband asked her, why she was crying. "Buffalo killed my father and I am a prisoner." "What about my people?" he asked. "We sacrificed our people to be with you and made a deal." Buffalo felt bad. He said, "Bring your father back to life; I will return you to your people."

She sang a song, "Magpie, Magpie, help me find a piece of father to mend back whole again." Magpie sat cocking his head to the side. She cried, "Magpie see what you can find." The maiden's song bent the grasses and the Magpie found a piece of her father, a bit of bone. She said it was enough and then laid the bone on the earth and covered it with her blanket.

She sang a song to revive her father, the song her grandmother taught her. Magpie and the young maiden looked underneath the blanket, but Hunter was not breathing. He was stone cold. She began singing softly and her father stood up; the buffalo marveled. They said, "Sing this song after every hunt and we will teach your people the buffalo dance. If you dance the buffalo dance before every hunt, your hunt will be a good one," they said, "If you sing this song for us, we will live again!" And the buffalo danced.

*****

The myth of the Blackfoot woman who married a dog was a favorite tale of the start of the Dog Society. The pretty maiden had many admirers. Indians used dogs to pull loads on travois. She borrowed her uncle's dog to haul wood. She loved the dog, which was obedient and liked her. She said to the dog, "If you were a young man I would marry you." That night, a young man came to her bed and covered her mouth briefly to prevent a scream. He was very gentle with her. That night she took charcoal as he slept and marked his back and hair. The next day, she saw the young men in the camp with no marks. Her uncle's dog came up to her and licked her hand with black marks on its head. This cannot be; I was with a human.

Again, that night the young man came to her in bed and they were together a long time. She had an idea and took his hand and bit him hard on the finger. The next day, there was a big dance. Her father was the chief. She asked him to have all of the braves in the village dance by her and extend their hands. They did, but none of them had a sore finger.

She strolled down by the lake. She thought, "I know I was with a young man." Then the dog limped up to greet her. It had an injured paw. "It is you who has been coming to my bed at night," she exclaimed. He turned into a handsome young man. He spoke and said, "It is your entire fault; you wished that I would become a young man and now I am." That evening, as it grew dark, the girl left her family lodge with food, clothes and supplies and met her young lover. The next day the girl and the dog gone.

Years passed and she, her husband and children returned to her uncle's lodge; she disguised herself. Her uncle asked how she knew the Blackfoot language. She said that her tribe was Blackfoot. He became suspicious when her husband took his meat outside and ate meat raw. Uncle arose early and saw the visitor asleep; his foot was uncovered and looked like a dog's paw. Uncle confronted them and the stranger admitted that he once was his dog and this woman was his brother's daughter. I have much medicine and that is how we came to be man and wife. Her parents were happy to have her back; they respected the dog's powers.

They pitched a lodge in the camp. Word circulated and the young men were jealous of the dog-man and his pretty wife and began to harass them and made rude comments. Things got worse. The young couple packed up and moved out of camp. The Dog-Man barked like a dog and all of the dogs in camp came running. He became Chief of the Dogs and the people had no dogs to haul their loads.

#30. Plains Sun Dancers
(Photograph Courtesy of Azusa Publishing, LLC)

## Chapter Seven
## Sun Dance and
## the Medicine Bundle

The Blackfoot Indians were sun-worshippers and believed in the Sun as their Creator God, called *Quilent-Sat-Men* and Mother Earth. *Ihsipaipiyo'pa* was the source of life or Creator God. *Apistaki* is the Blackfoot name for Great Spirit. They prayed to this deity to answer their prayers. The annual major ceremony of the Sun Dance festivity was the most important Blackfoot event of the year. By tradition, the Blackfoot, when the service berries (Saskatoon) were ripe in June during a full moon and the eternal light was shining down on the entire world. The tribal bands assembled for the "Sun Dance" in honor of the creator (the Sun), buffalo and the ancestors before them.

It was performed by dozens of Indian tribes; the Arapaho, Assiniboine, Cheyenne, Crow, Gros Ventre, Plains Cree, Sarsi, Sioux, Shoshoni, and Blackfeet tribes. All three tribes of the Blackfoot Confederacy held their own Sun Dances. The Sun Dance lasted about 12 days. The first four days were for travel and setting up camp.

There are many stories of the Sun Dance. Before the Sun Dance Ceremony, members of the Old Women's Society, called "Holy Women," built a holy ceremonial lodge, known as the "Sun Lodge," shaped like a buffalo corral. A few members wore buffalo headdresses, imitating the animal. Others wore an eagle feather and ermine tail headdress.

The Sun Dance was a religious ceremony for a promise to the Sun. If a warrior was spared death from the enemy, he might make a vow to the Sun-god to dance the Sun Dance. The Blackfoot made offerings to the Sun god, which they hung in trees or placed on a hillside. This practice was their religious duty. They sang offering songs to the Sun god, the supreme deity. His wife was the Moon and their son was the Morning Star.

On the day of the celebration, a sacred woman made a solemn vow to the sun god for the recovery of the sick. The woman, who was chosen to serve as medicine woman for the Sun Dance had to be true to her husband and had led a virtuous life to qualify to assume the role of making the solemn vow. The rites always began with the woman's vow, made to the Sun god for the recovery of the sick or for the safe return of a warrior husband or son from the war trail.

#31. Three Piegan Chiefs
(Photograph Courtesy of Azusa Publishing, LLC

The second day, the sacred woman began fasting. The ceremony began. They brought offerings for their prayers for sickness or to settle a family quarrel. Teepees were set up in a huge circle around the site where the Sun Lodge would be built; they wore their finest regalia and rode their very best horses. There was festivity and celebration as the Blackfoot prepared for the feast. The bands, clans and societies came from every direction. On the third day, buffalo tongues were cut and boiled for the sacred consumption. One hundred bull buffalo tongues were used in their sacred offering painted in stripes with red paint and prayers were uttered. They placed the cooked tongues in parcfletche bags.

The pipe and presents were given to the (*Omistaipokah*) lodge maker from the previous year. They smoked the pipe. The current presenters of the ceremony were given instruction by the last year's presenters and paid for their services. The woman donned the sacred bonnet.

The people assembled and a pole was cut; a tree for a sun pole for the center of the Sun Lodge was cut down and trimmed. The next day the ceremonial centre pole was raised. The Sun Lodge was built. The high priest or lodge builder was in charge. The Sun Lodge was a huge network of lodge poles, constructed to hold many in the arena. Three lodges were joined as one huge ceremonial Sun lodge. The fourth day, the 100-willow sweat lodge was constructed. Games and competitions were held.

The people assembled to fast and pray. Some made vows; others came for diversion. People chanted and gave incantations. Others sang sacred songs. There was dancing and singing, accompanied by drums, painted blue, green, red or yellow medicine eagle bone whistles, mariachis and buffalo hide rattles for the dance. The Blackfoot people danced in solemn celebration to their Sun god.

In the next four days, the camp was made ready. A feast was held. War bonnets trailed down the backs of the "Sun Chiefs," representing the buffalo's back. Warriors boasted about their great feats on the war trail. Women wore bright colored dresses and glass beads.

In the final four days, the Blackfoot performed the Sun Dance. The warriors wore breech clouts, and their bodies were painted. Sage was rubbed into their palms, and an attendant filled their pipes. The Sun Pole was a means of sacrifice and thanksgiving to the Sun god for answered prayers. The Blackfoot believed in self-mutilation for religious suffering.

Warriors entered to inflict self punishment on their bodies for vows to the Sun god to deliver them from danger, when they were surrounded by the enemy. They believed in self sacrifice for the suffering of the people. Thongs were attached to the top of the pole.

Warriors danced around the Sun Pole with thongs fastened at the top to pegs inserted into slits in their chests for self-affliction. Sometimes, buffalo skulls were inserted by thongs between the ropes and the pegs. The warriors strained to tear the skin, freeing the pegs, or had them cut out. They would perform the Sun Dance around the centre pole. They suffered from pain and exhaustion, but continued to dance. The scars on their chest were exhibited as trophies for the ordeal, and they would wear those scars for the rest of their lives. By the same rite a warrior chose self mutilation, by slashing his arms and legs before going on the war trail.

One type of self-sacrifice was self-torture performed by the warrior at night. In this case, the ordeal began at night as the sun went down and the warrior was released from the pegs, when the sun came up.

The *Okan* or Sun Dance is a sacred ceremony of prayer, renewal and sacrifice, the exalted Blackfoot Festival. Today, the ceremony lasts a day and a half. During the festivities, one hundred songs are sung.

Later, the women opened the medicine pipe bundle and the pipe was lit only by a service-berry stick or a buffalo chip. They smoked the pipe. In the "Sun Dance," only women priestesses were allowed to open the sacred bundles and call up the spirits. The Blackfoot smudged sweet grass incense bundles. The incense was burned on sacred alters. The Sun Dance was a "Rite of Intensification," because it was binding for the loosely organized tribal bands and was the only time of year that the whole tribe assembled. Ceremonies of the Plains culture were a time of festivity, dance, music and gaiety adorned with body paint, costumes and feathers.

The most exalted guest was the Sun Priest (holy man), who conducted and presided over the Sun Dance. The sacred pipe was smoked. The Blackfoot believed that the smoke and fragrance were transported into the heavens to their Sun god. The sun priests took the pipe by the stem and handed it to the next person in the same manner, to mimic the seizing of the bear. They smoked the "medicine pipe," and sang songs.

#32. Blackfeet Man & Woman
(Photograph Courtesy of Azusa Publishing, LLC)

The Brave Dogs emerged from their lodges in full regalia and took part in the Sun Dance by initiating the dance with a promenade. Brave Dogs led the procession, while the whole village followed behind them in dance. They danced to the pulsating drum beat and the shrill sounds of bone whistles, with religious fervor.    Both Buffalo and Gray Wolf dancers performed.    All of the members were painted. During the Sun Dance Ceremony, the Brave Dogs Society hung their weapons from the center lodge pole of the Sun Lodge, performing the rituals of the Sun Dance. Others sat in rows, observing.    They petitioned and prayed to the Sun god. The dancers were surrounded with feasting and gaiety.    The end of the ceremonies featured weather dancers and society dances.    The festivities concluded with the blessings of the medicine pipes and breaking camp.

*****

The Blackfoot "Medicine Pipe Society" was started long ago.    The legend tells how a man was struck by lightning and thunder. As he lay there, the Thunder Chief appeared to him in a vision and showed the man a wonderful pipe and instructed him to craft another like it.    The pipe was wrapped in white weasel skin with feathers attached. He was to make a medicine bundle from the skins of animals and birds to wrap the sacred pipe. One belief was for a sick person to make a vow and his health would return.

A grizzly bear appeared to the man and gave him his coat to wrap the bundle.    The bear told the man about the bundle transfer; he was to transfer early, while the bears were active.    It was important to have the man smoke the pipe and transfer the bundle.    No one could turn down a grizzly. A medicine bundle could be held for four years maximum.    A man was urged to sell the bundle and choose a solid person to pass the bundle to, giving feasts and ceremonials. The pipe was to be taken to visit a chief in his lodge.

In the spring, after the first thunder, the pipe was to be taken out and held up to the Sun god. The sacred Pipe was kept in a "Medicine Bundle." The pipe in Blackfoot society was all important.    One dance performed was the "Medicine Pipe Dance."    A medicine pipe was sacred, stored in the sacred bundle, handled by the women, who acted as "priestesses."    The Blackfoot recognized women as the foundation of humanity, accepted for the role in society.    Women, like priestesses, kept the sacred bundles used for ceremonies like the Pipe Dance.

**100**

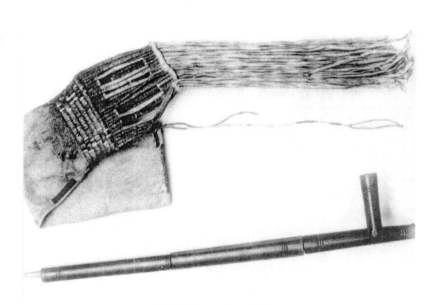

#33. Calumet Pipe & Bag
(Photograph Courtesy of Azusa Publishing, LLC)

The owl was featured in the pipe ceremony. The society sang owl songs when seeking a new candidate. They prayed to the owl that they could catch their victim sleeping. One night, when the camp was sound asleep, they were awakened by the sound of drums, singing and shouting. A herald announced the feast and asked that presents be brought to the buyer's lodge. The seller took the pipe, while the wives carried the medicine bundle.

The grand parade ended at the lodge of the buyer. The women placed the bundle on its holder at the rear of the lodge. The new owner of the bundle wore the ceremonial costume from the old owner. It had a buffalo skin headband and feathers in the hair, with a fringed beaded deerskin shirt and leggings with ermine tails, a blanket and moccasins.

In addition to the garb, the previous bundle owner passed on his horse, bridle, quirt and lariat. The former owner's wife also passed on her outfit to be worn during the pipe ceremony. People of the camp crowded around the lodge, leaving gifts. The gifts were given to the former owner in exchange for the medicine bundle, regalia, pipe and membership. In the actual swap, prayers, songs and dances were performed, and the animal skins from the sacred bundle were exchanged.

Sounds Imitating the prominent birds and animals were performed, including the buffalo, crane, grizzly, muskrat and owl. The ceremony ended as the old owner, buyer and his wife exited the lodge and prayed to the sun, four directions and mother earth. He instructed the new owner in prayers and rules for handling the sacred pipe. The new owner fasted and sought direction from the Sun god. Ownership was open to both sexes; new members were accepted.

The ceremony was accompanied with a feast. Songs were chanted, with the beat of the drum or tom-tom, along with the sounds of a charging bear. Another prominent figure of the Pipe ceremony was Owl. They chanted Owl songs and prayed to Owl for power. Thunder and Bear instructed them to wrap the medicine pipe in many skins of rawhide, feathers and weasel skins. The final wrap was the skin of the grizzly bear.

Drums accompanied the ceremony. A person from the village was invited to join the Medicine Pipe Society. He dared not refuse. He smoked the pipe and was brought a robe or blanket. They shared in paying for his dues to join. The new member was clothed in ceremonial dress. The pipe was paraded though camp. The ceremony lasted into the middle of the night. The society chanted as they marched behind. Certain rituals were performed while they entered the lodge. Drums were decorated with symbols of the sun, moon and stars. The beat imitated the drumming of the grouse. As the ceremony ended, the sacred pipe and bundle were returned to the ceremonial lodge. The other gifts were returned to the Pipe Society.

The "beaver bundle" could be purchased for a price, if the man made a vow to possess it. If the bundle sold, the seller had to teach the buyer the necessary dances, prayers, songs and drama. The warrior was believed to be able to forecast the weather by the moon and sky using the beaver bundle. With the magic bundle, one was believed to be able to call the buffalo herd to camp if food was low. A person that was ill was supposed to make a vow. The taboos dictated that the beaver was not to be killed or eaten.

Other Plains tribes held the Sun Dance. The Arapaho and Cheyenne were two Plains tribes that did, similar to the Blackfoot ceremony. The Arapaho and Cheyenne used the sacred medicine pipe bundle. The sacred bundle contained bison fur and four arrows, wrapped in animal skins and held powers. Nearly every Blackfoot warrior took his sacred bundle along for victory.

Sun Dance medicine paraphrenalia included buffalo hide rattles, a deerskin apron, an eagle bone whistle, a Sun Dance doll, and a lock of hair that was believed to cause a mist to cloak the warriors on a raid. The sacred items were to enable a vision, give special powers and long life.

The Blackfeet believed that their medicine bundles held mystical powers. Personal medicine bundles were employed to petition the Sun god to answer a prayer. The medicine bundle contained a sacred object like a stone or pipe. A warrior took his personal medicine bundle on the war trail to bring victory in battle and in taking horses from the enemy on a raid.

Medicine war shields were adorned with painted symbols and bedecked with feathers. The medicine war shield was big magic on the war path. A Shaman used his medicine bundle in healing the sick. Medicine bundles were used in love, healing and on the hunt. A personal rawhide medicine amulet bag containing herbs, a seashell or other sacred objects was worn around the neck as a good omen.

Purification was an important part of the Blackfoot life and their religion. It was necessary to be cleansed before the Sun Dance. One way was the sweat lodge. There, the men to bathe and communicate. The lodge was a willow hut, covered with thatch, leaving a smoke vent at the top. There was a central fire pit surrounded by rocks. Hot coals were brought in to ignite the logs. Water sprinkled on the burning logs produced the steam. Sage or sweet grass scattered over the coals acted as incense.

#34. Lookout
(Photograph Courtesy of Azusa Publishing, LLC)

**104**

The bathers sat with their heads between their knees, breathing in the warm vapor from the bath. Prayers and incantations were uttered by those bathing. They felt the purity and felt cleansed of evil spirits. The experience allowed their Creator to send them a vision. They believed that their Sun god was the source of all power and life.

The braves contemplated life and prayed to their Creator. The central fire pit represented the core of the universe. The fire, rock, and water were symbols of life. To them, all things held life, given by the Creator. The rocks symbolized Grandmother Earth, from which nature emerged. Fire used to heat the rocks symbolized the rays from the Sun god to warm the earth and stimulate growth. The fire-logs came from the stately trees. The water reminded them of pure, swift flowing streams. All of these things were attributed to their celestial Creator. At the end of the session, the men all ran down and submerged in a cold lake or stream.

The cleansing and purity led to the challenge of the young brave to perform his all-important vision-quest. The Blackfoot brave had to complete a series of feats to attain manhood. He was to observe to be groomed in archery, dancing, hunting, running, swimming, and trailing to become a man.

Religion tied into nature through dreams or visions involving a bird or animal and was much a part of the brave attaining manhood. Counting coup, the vision quest, owning the medicine pipe bundle, and join a society were all steps to becoming a man in their culture

The path of the brave to become a man was to master a vision quest, have a vision and gain a name, to touch the enemy and count coup. The vision quest was one of self-sacrifice, supplication, fasting and danger. The brave was to fast and pray, go on a raid, steal a horse and become a war party's helper. The young warrior was to become a scout and then a leader of scouts before he became a pipe holder. Braves joined a society.

A young Blackfeet woman first sought purification in a sweat lodge, before she lamented and prayed to the Creator and ascended a hill top, in order to receive her vision. She also cleansed herself for the vision-quest, the menstrual hut and child bearing.

The Sun Dance ranked highest of any Blackfeet celebration. This festivity was more important than other events. Their religion and the worship of the Sun god, Creator was felt in every fiber of their existence and involved their sacrifice. Prayers, incantations and supplications were uttered to their Creator. The people anticipated the gaiety, laughter, friendship, singing, dancing and visiting during the gala festivities.

**105**

#35. Bear **Bull.** Blackfeet Elder, Societal Member
(Photograph Courtesy of Azusa Publishing, LLC)

# Chapter Eight
## Sacred Societies

Societies among the Blackfoot Indians were a cult organization and a way of life for both sexes, a mix of religious beliefs similar to fraternities. Societies were common on the Northwestern Plains. They infiltrated from tribe to tribe, as well as societal names, over time.

If societies had a known geographic center and origin, it cannot be ascertained. It seems logical that societal culture spread from tribe to tribe through alliances and intertribal marriage. Each society was unique to its own tribe. The names of societies were usually a totem of an animal like the bear, mountain lion, or wolf. The totem is a symbol of hierarchy in ideals.

There were numerous hunting societies; hunting bands were formed of 20 to 30 families comprising 80 to 120 twenty men, women and children. Bands were formed of extended families.

Blackfoot societies were ranked by importance. Function of the society was for tribal council, war, hunting and so on. At the top was the tribal council. Next was the military society followed by the hunting society. Military societies were purchased by the individual. They were war societies, often named after an animal, like the Kit-fox and a Dog society.

Blackfoot societies were the Dogs, Bad Horn (Blackfoot), Bees, Black Soldiers (Bloods), Braves, Brave Dogs, Crazy or Mad Dogs, Bulls, Catchers, Doves, Flies, Grizzly Bear Braves, Kit-foxes, Mosquitoes, Prairie Chickens, Ravens, Soldiers, Tails, Ugly Horn, and the Water Braves.

There was also a Cow Buffalo Society for women, a Bear Cult, and a Tobacco Society. Some societies existed in all of the tribes of the Blackfoot Nation. The Bull Society was named for the buffalo. The name of the great chief, Sitting Bull, in the Sioux tongue meant buffalo bull. Local matters were taken care of by camp police appointed by the tribal head chief. Tribal police patrolled the camp at night, kept order and regulated functions.

A tribe might have a number of societies. There were societies for the older men ranked down to the young braves, barely 15 years of age. Children, younger than 15 years old were not eligible for cults. At 15, braves were considered old enough to go to war. Young men began in the lowest society, but they worked into higher societies. Moving up from a youth society involved smoking the pipe and asking for an elder's clothes. The brave was summoned to a ceremonial lodge where he received new clothes and his body was painted. He was then accepted into the society.

With the ordeal, there was plenty of dancing and music; each brave shot his bow and arrows. All of this represented his passing into manhood in order to become a warrior. Younger men joined age group societies that imitated the regalia, dance and song of the elders. Young braves were ranked by age grading. They were grouped in age brackets like 15-18 and 19-23, etcetera. The braves worked up in grade and rank by maturity. Societies, as a whole, were called, All Comrades.

The Fly Society was the first young men's society of members at 20 years of age. Lay members in the pageant were painted red and yellow with stripes painted across their eyes and noses. They also wore buffalo robes and a downy eagle feather on their head; an eagle claw hung from their wrist to designate the proboscis of the fly. Chief of Flies wore a downy eagle feather on his head and a yellow buffalo robe and was painted like the rest.

The ceremonial dance of the Flies was performed as they knelt in a circle around the singers. They danced in celebration. They ducked their heads and made grunting noises like buffalo. They sang four songs before rushing out to claw at the tribe's people, imitating the Flies. The people acted afraid and ran from them. The celebration lasted four days. Other Plains tribes had the Mosquito societies. Fly societies and Mosquito societies were similar. The last ceremony was held in 1872.

The Mosquito Society formed among the Blackfoot and was compiled of young braves. They were painted for the occasion and sang and danced in their costumes. They had one leader, four old man comrades, four yellow mosquitoes, two single man comrades, a number of mosquitoes and four drummers. They were painted nearly the same as the Flies and sang and danced to the festivities.

The Dove Society began among the Piegan in 1855 and spread into the Blackfoot and Blood Tribes, a young brave's organization that rose from the dream of a Piegan man. The Dove Society was initiated and a chief was elected. A double ceremonial lodge was constructed and was used for feasts and dances. The candidates, dressed in breech clout and moccasins, and given a puff of smoke from the pipe of a Dove member.

Each was presented with a new bow, arrows and buffalo calf quiver, which they later shot outside. The ceremony lasted three days. They joined the other candidates and sat outside in a line facing the Sun god. Singers chanted to the beat of drums and sang Dove songs and were summoned into the lodge where the candidate's face and body were painted. They received new garb and were accepted in the society.

#36. Nez Perce Chief Joseph
Fought the Blackfeet until 1855
(Photograph Courtesy of Azusa Publishing, LLC)

Societies, like the Kit-foxes were common in many Plains tribes, but did not perform the same ceremony. Native religion could not separate the societal cults and their way of life. These war groups had their own costumes, dances, insignias and songs. War societies defended the camp against possible enemy attack. Warrior societies acted as an advance or a rear guard when moving to a new camp location or as the guard on ceremonial hunts. Their general duty was to maintain order and punish offenders.

The Kit-fox Society was one of the earliest Blackfoot societies and originated in a dream of a Piegan warrior called Elk-tongue, who dreamed of a Kit-fox (while on an expedition of war against the Shoshoni Indians). The fox came to him in a dream and invited Elk-tongue into his den, where he and his mate were seated. He saw two lances wrapped in skin, fringed with feathers and two lances on the other wall wrapped in swan skins, adorned with feathers. The fox showed Elk-tongue their dance and how to dress for the occasion and told the old warrior how to always wear a fox skin on his back to be used as medicine, only that it was bad for any other reason. The sly one directed him to form a Kit-fox Society from a group of their young braves in his village. He was to teach them to dress and dance.

As legend tells us, the Kit-fox Society was formed. The young warriors wore deerskin war shirts, breech clouts, leggings, and moccasins. The Kit-fox Society called for special adornment and regalia; the leader wore a fox skin and headpiece with four eagle feathers and a foxtail with bells attached. The fox headpiece had brass buttons for the eyes and a red cloth tongue. The leader carried bow and arrows in a mountain lion skin quiver. The assistants were painted blue and red. The members wore otter skin bands on their arms and ankles.

The Dogs entered the ceremonial lodge and gave the Kit-fox members a filled pipe to smoke. Wives of the Kit-fox painted the Dog Society wives. The society members sat in the first row, their wives behind them. Outgoing members sat in the second row. Then, they chewed an herb and sang songs.

The Kit-fox leader led the dance to the drums; he was followed by his officers. The members danced behind them. Dancers feigned having trouble removing their lances, which were stuck in the ground. They removed them and began their dance in pairs to mimic foxes.

#37. Chief Iron Breast in **Bull** Society Attire
(Photograph Courtesy of Azusa Publishing, LLC)

The pair barked and hopped, with their feet close together in a zigzag pattern, like a fox. As they danced, the members hopped like foxes, danced and held their spears in the air. The leader would announce a break. The warriors would return to their seats for a brief time and then resume dancing. The sacred festivities lasted four sessions of four consecutive nights

The fifth day, they came out of the ceremonial lodge. The leader was adorned with his fox skin and headdress. His body was painted red and his face green. He held a bow and arrows that were painted green and caused fear in the hearts of the people. One assistant had a curved staff wrapped in otter skin and eagle feathers and the other's lance was wrapped in swan skin, bedecked with eagle feathers and painted. They wore eagle feathers on the back of their heads. Otter skin anklets, with bells were worn by the members. The band marched through the village, giving out war whoops at random. The society formed a fox head; the leader was the nose. The assistants were the eyes and the society formed the head to end the pageantry.

Before Elk-tongue died, he taught his son the secrets of the Kit-fox Society: dance and medicine. In the smallpox epidemic of 1841, all of the members in the Kit-fox Society perished, except one. He passed the medicine of the Kit-fox Society onto the Horn Society of the Piegan, Blood and Blackfoot tribes.

Legend tells us that the Gros Ventre Indians did not allow one of their chiefs to join their society. Out of revenge, the scorned chief relayed the secrets of the Brave Dog Society to head Chief, White Calf, of the Bloods.

Blackfoot warriors could change their names after every coup. Some warriors had more than one name. In this time period, there were two chiefs named White Calf; one was a Blood tribesman and the other a Piegan. In addition, there was a Blood chief, Calf Shirt, as well as a Piegan named Chief Calf Shirt.

The Braves (All-Tried Warriors) Societies were the most powerful after 1850. The Braves Society came from a dream of a tribesman. He referred to his dream as a "strong dream." He described the vision as being like dogs watching over the camp, intermingling with braves.

The leader wore a coyote skin and was called "the Wolf-skin Man." He wore a war shirt, tail and carried a gourd rattle. He wore war paint and carried a painted lance with feathers. The right half of his face was painted blue. The left side was painted red. His assistant was called Willow Brave. He wore a hairless buffalo robe with buffalo hoof rattles that jangled.

The symbol of the Brave Dog Society was a red sash of trade cloth, eight inches wide and about seven feet long. The sash was decorated with eagle feathers and had a slit to insert the members' head. It was called a dog rope. A black hood was worn, made from a piece of smoked teepee skin. This was adorned with red feathers. A tail of red cloth and owl feathers hung down as the raven's tail. Each member carried a deerskin-covered rattle. Their bodies were adorned in a bright painted design. The dance followed. There was a presentation of gifts by the leader's wife and family.

The Brave Dog Society varied from the norm. Their pageantry involved a leader, assistants and horsemen. There were four old man comrades, two single man comrades, two bear all Brave Dogs, four drummers, and 20 All Brave-dogs.

There were White Braves with white painted lances and bone whistles. Burning sage was stuck into the ground. Their bodies were painted white with four black or yellow stripes painted across their eyes and noses. Black stripes were painted on their arms, calves and thighs. The White Braves carried an eagle feather. Two members acted as water and pemmican carriers.

The Piegan Brave Dog Society bundle held a whip and a war bridle used for their horses. When not in use, the bundle hung from a pole in the society lodge. The society buffalo hide rattle hung from another pole with an ermine tail banner, an eagle feather war bonnet and a suit of weasel tails.

When camp was moved, they beat their drums and sang. At night they curled up in a pack in the center of camp. When they continued on, the society remained behind, cleaned up the camp and ate the remaining food, like dogs. They followed to the new campsite and arrived late; after the lodges were pitched and the fires were started.

The Brave Dogs lasted until 1874, when they sold their society to younger members. In 1925, much older past members held a Raven Bearers Dance. The Braves Society acted as the scouts who went out and located the buffalo herds. They guarded the herd and its location. If anyone stampeded the herd, the Braves caught them. They were severely whipped and their clothes removed. That way, when the guilty parties came into camp naked and bruised, they were shamed.

#38. Blackfeet Caravan
(Photograph Courtesy of Azusa Publishing, LLC)

114

Each society had a different name, ceremony and dance. There were songs and drum accompaniment. Weapons and feathers were displayed. Braves were clad only in breech clouts and moccasins. They sometimes wore a buffalo robe as part of the ceremony.

In the play, they acted out the role of the animal represented, like the fly or mosquito or a brave fete or battle. They sat in a group with the leader, drummers, members and candidates. The more militant were fully armed or just carried a spear. The last dance of the Braves was held in 1877.

The Grizzly Braves carried bow and arrows instead of lances. The Grizzly Bears imitated the grizzly. Their faces were painted red and black in what they called a "bear-faced pattern." It entailed black vertical lines painted across the eyes.

Members wore bear skin headdresses, complete with their vesture adorned with bear claws, ears, fringed buckskin shirt, and their bodies painted with bright colors. Rattles were carried, as well as eagle feathers. They had their own dance and routine. Each member carried a buffalo hide shield. The Grizzly Bear Braves were a war society.

The Black Soldiers were a Blood Society. The idea of the society came from a dream of a Blackfoot warrior. He described seeing a vision of Black Soldiers wearing the regalia of narrow wolf skin head bands with two eagle feathers attached with wolf skin anklets and wrist bands. Two vertical lines were painted on the cheeks to represent wolf teeth. Black bands were painted across the forehead and chin. The entire body was painted red as were the lances, which had strips of wolf skin attached.

The leader wore a wolf skin across his shoulders and carried a wooden war club, with a single feather. The Black Soldiers formed a circular mass and rotated slowly as the leader moved outside in the opposite direction. They sang and mimicked the wolf bark and call, and danced (to imitate the wolf), shaking their lances as the song ended.

The Black Soldiers often acted as camp police on their annual camp moves. If a member missed a ceremony, the society cut his teepee and apparel to shreds with their lances. Sometimes they beat the offender on the head and shoulders if a meeting was missed. The Royal Canadian Mounted Police issued an order that the Black Soldiers had no right to use punishment. The society existed until 1890.

The Soldier Society resembled the Black Soldiers, acting as police, but the Soldiers were more a healing society and not military. The Soldier Society was more severe in punishment than the Black Soldiers Society, and used tomahawks at times to discipline offenders.

The "medicine bundle" was a sacred religious article that contained treasured objects revered by the tribe, with the ability to control the destiny of the owner. The object was displayed only on special occasions.

The personal bundle itself was made of many different skins of birds and animals that were wrapped around a sacred object, such as a medicine pipe or other object. The sacred bundle was hung in the lodge behind where the owner slept and was considered to have great influence on his dreams. The sacred medicine bundle had much effect on the membership in societies. The power from the spiritual world was believed to come from the sacred medicine bundle, which was taken into war to insure victory.

A Medicine Pipe Bundle might contain various animal and bird skins, as well as other objects. There were various kinds of medicine bundles: the Sun Dance Bundle, War Medicine Bundle, Medicine Pipe Bundle and Beaver Bundle. The Sun Dance Bundle was opened during the Sun Dance Ceremony or Medicine Lodge Ceremony.

War Medicine Bundles were taken to the battlefield to assure victory in war. Sacred symbols on teepees were linked to the bundles and powers in battle. The Medicine Pipe Bundle was opened at the first sound of thunder in the spring and during the Medicine Pipe Ceremony or if someone vowed to attend the Sun Dance. The Beaver Bundle was used in conjunction with a good tobacco harvest and in calling the buffalo. The bundle was also opened when it was transferred to a purchaser.

Social dances performed were the Begging Dance, Grass Dance, Kissing Dance, Night Singers Dance and the Tea Dance. The Black-tailed Deer Dance was a good hunting dance. They performed the "Horse Dance" and the "War Dance," both war dances. Religious dances were the Sun Dance and Ghost Dance, which invited the dead, not to be confused with the Ghost Shirt Dance.

A Nez Perce prophet, *Smohalla,* proclaimed that Indians would rise from the dead and drive the white-eyes out of the land, initiating the Dreamer's Religion. Wavoca, a Paiute holy man in Nevada, called Jack Wilson, had a vision of immortal warriors in painted Ghost shirts with sacred symbols dancing in a circle invincible to white man's bullets in "the Ghost Shirt Religion" (*Natdia,* in Paiute).

Word from Nevada spread to the Plains, reaching the Sioux about the Ghost Dance religion. The Arapaho, Cheyenne and Sioux accepted the Ghost Shirt Religion and the Ghost Dance. Late one night in 1890, young Sioux warriors danced the Ghost Dance in their sacred shirts around a blazing campfire and fired their rifles into the air, giving war-whoops, frightening nearby settlers, at Wounded Knee. The U.S. Cavalry came the following day, and to set an example, Sioux Chief Sitting Bull was shot and killed. Sitting Bull's death marked the passing of an era.

Many Indian tribes surrendered to Colonel Miles in his 1876-77 Campaign, but the Brule and Oglala Sioux at Pine Ridge resisted. After the Ghost Dance incident in 1890, the Sioux were ambushed by the U.S. Seventh Cavalry and Buffalo Soldiers at Wounded Knee in South Dakota Territory. Hundreds of Sioux Indians were massacred. The Medicine Man's dream became a nightmare. Sioux Chief Big Foot surrendered to the Army.

The society emblem was kept in a bundle. Painted yellow sticks, with bow and arrows, a yellow calf tail and buffalo calf hooves were in the sacred bundle. The sticks were used to discipline disobedient tribes-people. The society leader and his officers were keepers of the pipe and two other assistants were in charge of the bow and arrows.

In the dance, each member carried a punishing stick, moving it up toward the Sun god and down, as if to draw the powers down to mother earth. The people were careful not to miss dances or be punished. A staged scenario was for a warrior in his best attire on his horse and fine saddle blanket near the dancers. The society would act like they shook him up and cut his clothes and blanket to shreds. Their actions were to gain the respect of the tribe and maintain order. The well being of the village was put first.

The Bulls was not an All Comrades Society. It was a company of elders in the tribe. Around 1820, an old warrior had a dream while on a hunting trip. He observed a certain dance in his dream and heard the songs. The old warrior sold the society to a party of older men and taught them the dance, songs and gave them the cult insignia. Some Bulls members wore eagle feather headdresses that stood straight up; another type of headdress was the scalp from the buffalo skull and horns. Members of the order wore buffalo robes, the fur side out. Two of the warriors wore the robes of an aged buffalo, which they called these "Scabby Bulls." White clay was rubbed on the fur as mud. Leaders wore upright eagle feather bonnets, with an arrow suspended horizontally, about eye level, with dyed red eagle plumes at either end. Weasel skin strips were hung from the shaft as fringe.

The Bulls lived around a lake away from camp. They would announce the intention to dance. They emerged from their lodges, pre-dressed and painted, to begin the ceremony. The Bulls lay in the grass, with three buffalo robes over them, imitating the herd. The leader commissioned a loner to approach. He threw a pebble into the water to scare the buffalo. They stood up, but lay back down. The lone warrior took buffalo chips and started them on fire and set them afloat in the lake. They floated atop the water and the smoke drifted toward the Bulls. The Bulls stirred and the rider rode toward them, shouting and giving war whoops.

He began moving the herd toward the camp (this represented moving a herd over a buffalo jump). He led them to the place of the dance, and the people surrounded the buffalo. The herder recounted how he had found the herd and captured them, counting coup.

The Bulls crouched down under their robes and sang four songs. As they sang the dance song, the Bulls arose to dance. They danced, imitating the movements of the buffalo. The Bulls Society was short lived. When they gave the last performance of the buffalo jump, an elder member was injured and died. It was the end of an era. The Bulls were regarded as a religious society, whose job was to locate the buffalo for the camp to hunt.

Legend placed the Ugly Horn Society, early pre 1800. Like most Blackfoot societies, the Ugly Horn (Bad Horn) society arose from a dream of an Indian warrior or shaman. His dream was described as having two leaders with fringed leggings and a fringed garment and moccasins.

The vesture was a buffalo robe with a loose fitting hood adjoined to the garment. The hood consisted of painted staffs and circles, cut out for eyes and mouth, with flaps on the sides for ears. The two leaders wore buffalo robes, with buffalo hoof rattles.

Two stories revealed the origin of the Tails. In the first tale, it seems a Blackfoot woman, whose people were starving, found a talking buffalo stone. It instructed her that they should sing certain songs, and perform the dance and rituals. They did this, and consequently, a buffalo herd was called to their camp and the famine was over.

In addition, the woman learned how to make a buffalo jump and gave this knowledge to the tribe. In the buffalo jump, a medicine man waved a blanket and shouted or started a fire that drove the frightened buffalo over a cliff, called a "buffalo jump or fall." The animals were put out of their misery.

She had also learned how to build a buffalo corral with built-up lanes, in a v-shape.  The buffalo were lured by a decoy or driven into the corral and slaughtered.

In the other folk story regarding the origin of the Tails in the Blackfoot legend, it describes how long ago, a woman was carried away by a buffalo to another village, where they had two ceremonial lodges adjoined.  The buffalo removed their coats and they appeared just like humans.  The woman's captor took her for a wife and revealed all of the society secrets.  She remained nearly a year and then returned to her village.  She introduced the two societies.  The Tails Society had two leaders and a pipe keeper; there were an unknown number of tails and four drummers, also Old Man Comrades and Single Men Comrades.  There were also female members.

The Catcher Society had two leaders and a number of catchers.  They had two Pipe Men and four drummers.  There were two Tomahawk Men and several dozen women members.  The society was purely Piegan and ranked one higher than the Kit-fox Society.  Every member carried a cherry wood club, about 30" long, painted red with a hawk or eagle feather and a buffalo hoof rattle.  A piece of otter skin, with an eagle feather, was worn in the hair at the back of the head.  Their shirts were painted red.

The officers carried quivers with arrows.  Two young men were picked as keepers of the tomahawk-pipes.  They wore buffalo robes with a large beaded brass cross in the center.

Kit-foxes, that were ready to move up and become Catchers, built two combined lodges for their ceremony central to the camp circle.  Members of the Dogs gave the filled pipe to the Catcher.  Catchers painted the Dogs.  Two young men were picked as messengers and keepers of the tomahawk-pipes and wore buffalo robes.  Instruction was given for the dance in the Lodge and the members, and then the candidates filed outside.  The new members danced, facing out then in, intermittently.  They danced four dances in succession.  Night meetings consisted of a feast in the double lodge given by a female Catcher member.  Dancing and song lasted four days.  The last Catcher Society ceremony was performed circa 1850.

This story from legend, tells how the Raven Bearers Society began.  An old warrior was critically wounded in battle and his companions had to leave him there.   Shot in the leg, for many days the old warrior lay unconscious.  When he awoke, the old man had a vision of a flock of ravens flying overhead.

He heard a raven in a bush just next to him. The raven spoke to him and told him that he was safe and would not die. In his vision, the Raven Chief called the other ravens to come and dance. The ravens made a circle around the raven chief and became like men. They commenced to sing and dance. The raven chief carried a flag with many feathers. He told the old warrior to observe them and take the memory home. The old warrior gathered the needed special feathers and costumes and made a flag and added raven feathers to it. He organized the Raven Bearer Society.

The leader of the Raven Bearers wore the complete preserved raven, feathers and all, as an ornament on his head. Porcupine quills adorned the wings and a strip of red flannel served as the tongue. The Raven Bearers danced in a circle and faced the inside of the circle. They all held their staffs upward and croaked, imitating the sounds of ravens. The leader turned to face out. The members all sat down and rose to resume the dance.

The Horn Society (Bloods) was an old religious cult, not an Age Society. The society was formed by the women's Buffalo Cows society, by a woman, named *Ma'toki*. They danced annually at the Sun Dance.

A story about the origin of the Horn Society went like this. A man married a Buffalo Cow, who ran away and rejoined her herd. She became a human and her calf a son. The son founded the Horn Society to prolong the dance of the buffalo calves.

Cult members were elders of religious rank. The people feared their having powers over life. Horn members took a pledge to tell the truth and live right, when they smoked the pipe. Two leaders wore breech-clouts, war shirts, leggings, and war bonnets that had horns and tails.

The leader of the dances wore an arrow shaft across the front of his headdress, about eye-level. The next member in rank wore a headpiece with buffalo horns, trimmed with ermine fur, dangling on either side. A lower officer wore a deerskin shirt, leggings and a swanskin cap, with a yellow staff, sharpened on one end, with black and white flannel fringe.

Four Scabby Bulls wore bonnets with horns and buffalo cow robes, hair side out. The leader wore a snake bonnet painted yellow, with beaded zigzag lines and plumes on both sides. Two members wore four owl feathers in their hair and carried an eight-foot lance. One lance was wrapped with swan skin, the other with otter skin.

Lay members wore breech clouts, moccasins, and a broad band headdress with feathers. Their bodies were adorned with war paint. Horn members had a single row of feathers over the top of the bonnet, accented with horse hair that represented the buffalo's back. A red feather plume started the row and a red trade cloth tail hung in back.

The duty of the Horn Society was to cut, drag in and erect the center lodge pole for the Sun Lodge. The religious cult prayed that the tree fall straight and true. The cult was upheld in religious standing. Sacred ceremonies were held in double lodges for important events.

Costumed summer dance leaders, put fear in the hearts of the children. They offered to carry the bad children off to the mountain tops if they were not obedient to their parents. The parents received a pledge from them to be good for another year, which cemented relationships and strengthened the bond. The Horn dance mimicked the movements of buffalo calves. The dance united their god's healing with the people on earth.

Love replaced evil. A person could not strike another person or he was killed. A person could not strike an animal on the skull when butchering or face retribution. Ridiculous rules, resembling wife's tales, were enforced. Striking an animal's spine could cause back problems. Pipes were to be extinguished with the fingers or the offender might experience sore eyes. Burning animal or human hair in a lodge caused dizziness or insanity and burning feathers in a lodge caused chaos. Stirring food with a knife caused one's teeth to fall out. Eating waterfowl causes a sore face.

Each constituent owned a pipe and smoked it in ceremonies. The pipe was short with a stone head, and had a sweet grass braid attached. The main object exchanged in the transfer of a membership ceremony was the pipe. Displacement was the only means of membership transfer. The rules of the Horn Society stood as the law in the village.

Candidates could trade for regalia and join the cult. They believed that a man coming to a Horn member could say that he was ill and make a vow and receive healing. He would then take the constituent's place as a candidate and could attend the next meeting. The seller sold his medicine pipe bundle to a new candidate for a rich sum; then, they were considered friends. The Horn Society was nearly wiped out in 1850: by 1925, only 25 members remained. Much of the ritual has now been lost.

The Bear Cult (Bloods) was first founded by a lad who claimed to have lived among the bears. Two members, called Bear Braves wore bear skin sashes, with eagle feathers and bear claws. Bits of bear skin served as ears and two black vertical lines represented bear's teeth.

Four leaders were referred to as White Braves; each carried a bone whistle. Each yielded a short spear with owl feathers attached, and a broad steel knife affixed to serve as a spearhead and eagle feathers at the base. Two members, called Black Bags carried the pemmican.

Red Braves yielded wooden shafts with a metal knife affixed to it. The staffs were wrapped in four places with strips of red trade cloth. The White Braves' staffs were wrapped in four places with swan skin. Bear Braves had two arrows. One arrow was pointed on the end and the other had a clump of bear skin affixed to it and was sinew wrapped.

The society performed by moving in four circular movements with arrows pointed in the direction of the sun. They shot their bear skin tipped arrows high in the air. Anyone struck by an arrow became a Bear member. The Bear dance began as the Bears sat on the east side, with White Bear Braves on the south, and the others faced the Bear Braves.

Red Braves and Black Bear Braves stuck their staffs into the ground, as did the White Braves. Bears sat with their heads covered with buffalo robes. It was then that the young males ran around the Bears pelting them with dried horse droppings. The Bears, acting angry arose, dropped their robes and growled loudly, and then sat down, covering their heads with buffalo robes. The youth's pelted them again. They sprang up with their bows and arrows and danced in a circle. White Braves replaced them in dance, blowing their bone whistles, while others danced in their stead.

The Bears moved to their left in front of the main body and pretended to shoot arrows at the Red Braves at the Black Bag's feet (the two members carrying the pemmican), forcing them back. The White Braves circled the crowd, to where they had been before. They retreated from the Bears. The Bears again shot their arrows into the air before they returned to their seats and sat down. Food was stacked in the center, but could not be eaten until a signal from the Bears. The Bears rushed to the Black Bag and began to devour the pemmican. Then they fed the spectators. The sacred Bear Society was a healing cult and received powers from the Sun god. The Bear Cult existed until circa 1925.

The Bear Cult members possessed "Medicine Knife Bundles" and employed these weapons in war. The knife was a double-edged metal dagger with a broad wooden handle and a feather and bell ornament attached. The Bear Knife Bundle could be sold or used in ceremonies. The bundle was exchanged in a ceremony where the purchaser's face was painted red, while scratch marks were indicated on the painted cheeks by the seller. Painting vertical black lines below the eyes as bear teeth transferred power to the new owner.

The Tobacco Society used a sacred "Beaver Medicine Bundle." The Blackfoot believed that the Tobacco Society and the Beaver Bundle were received about the same time period from the "Dwarf People," who were overseers of the tobacco gardens. The Blackfoot humored the little people by leaving them food and clothing outside of their lodges, and leaving prayers to them for a good tobacco crop.

The Beaver Ceremony was held when the tobacco seeds were planted and the beavers left their dens. A double lodge was constructed and the Tobacco Society assembled there. The whole village attended. The festivities lasted from dusk to dawn. The custodian's wife opened the bundle. She unwrapped the otter skin and tied it to a long pole and leaned it against the lodge. They began to dance with a stick encased in a small moccasin.

The young men assembled outside of their lodge and were told to wet their sticks. They were systematically fed by sticking their sticks into the lodge. Meat was stuck onto the point of the sticks for their consumption.

The custodian led the group in prayers and song as the preceded to the site of the tobacco crop. He started a fire to burn off the grass and weeds for a good garden spot. Before retiring, the camp people put out the fire and prayed for a good bumper crop of tobacco.

Fertilizer was placed in a rawhide bag with chokecherries, service berries and water. There was dancing, songs, and prayers for a prosperous yield, while sweet grass was burned. The custodian used a planting stick to insert holes in the ground in a line for the seeds. Each society member planted his own row of tobacco.

They returned to camp and were not allowed to watch the work of the little dwarfs. A boy was sent to check on the crop. If his report was good, the members checked it out, too. The Indians were so superstitious, that if their row failed, they expected illness or a death in the family. The best tobacco was saved back for the societies. Tobacco was never smoked pure, but mixed with leaves and bark to make kinnikinnnick.

During Buffalo Days, the Blackfoot Confederacy had numerous war societies, like the Braves, Bulls, Horns, Crazy Dogs and Kit Foxes with their own customs, rites, songs and dances. A new candidate was required to be brave, generous, honest and truthful to join. These societies still continue to this day.

123

#39. Kit Carson Army
Scout, Fur Trapper And
Indian Fighter

124

## Chapter Nine
### White Man Intervention

In the 17th Century, Europeans began arriving in North America east of the Mississippi. Western America remained a wilderness. By 1800, few Americans had been west of the Mississippi. At the turn of the 19th Century, the western frontier remained a wilderness, inhabited mostly by Indians and animals. Thomas Jefferson became President in 1801. He sent a secret message to Congress urging that trade be established with the Indians. He urged them to raise livestock, grow crops and enter into manufacturing.

In 1803, Jefferson signed papers of the Louisiana Purchase from France. With one stroke of the pen, he signed the Louisiana Purchase and doubled the size of America, gaining the territory west of the Mississippi to the Rocky Mountains between Canada and Mexico for $15,000,000. Jefferson was interested in the land west of the Rockies to the Pacific Ocean. He asked Congress for monies for an expedition to the Pacific Ocean. Congress responded with a mere $2,500 to bankroll it. President Thomas Jefferson authorized the military expedition of Captain Meriwether Lewis and Captain William Clark in 1803 to lead an expedition of the Corp of Discovery with 31 army corps and hired men cross-country to the Pacific Ocean, opening up a whole new hemisphere for western expansion.

The Corp journeyed from St. Louis to the upper Missouri River Valley region of what is now North Dakota. Lewis and Clark reached the Sioux-speaking Mandan Village on the north bank of the Missouri River. At that time, Toussaint Charbonneau, a French-Indian fur trapper, greeted them. They hired him as an interpreter and met his wife, Sacajawea or "Bird Woman," in the Shoshoni language.

The Lewis and Clark party spent the winter of 1804 in Fort Mandan, where Sacajawea bore Charbonneau a son, who was named Baptiste. In the spring of 1805, they left Fort Mandan and canoed the Missouri River through "grizzly country," to its headwaters.

In June of 1805, Lewis and Clark neared the Rocky Mountains, beyond the Great Falls of the Missouri River. This was Blackfoot Country. They would cross 1,000 miles of uncharted wilderness. Along the Missouri, the Blackfoot stole seven of Lewis and Clark's best horses. At one point, Lewis and Clark had to use firearms against the Blackfoot Indians. This was the only case of American Indians being hostile towards them. The party circumvented the Blackfoot after that, avoiding them.

According to William Clark, a war party of Shoshoni had killed two Gros Ventre warriors in the Bear Paw Mountains and stole a white pony. The Shoshoni later met a party of Piegan Blackfoot Indians. The Shoshoni made peace with the Blackfoot's and gifted them the pony. The Gros Ventre, who had always been their allies, later saw the same white horse in the Piegan camp. They thought that the Blackfoot had killed their tribesmen and declared war on them. For five years, they violently fought each other. The Blackfoot had few allies and a host of enemies. They seemed to thrive on war. The Sarsi tribe in Canada was a close ally. The Gros Ventre (Atsina, Hidatsa or the Big Belly) tribe had been allies for years before the white horse incident.

John Colter signed on with the Lewis and Clark Expedition and trekked with the party to Astoria near the Pacific Ocean in 1803. Colter had a friend in the corps named John Potts; both were privates and nearly the same age. In 1806, the party, under Lewis, started back east. They traveled overland past the falls of the Missouri River. The Lewis and Clark party had divided a short time for exploration. Lewis took a party down the Missouri River.

While exploring the Marias River, they encountered eight Piegan warriors. George Drouillard spoke to them in Indian Sign Language. They shared their camp with the Indians that night and a guard was posted. Early the next morning, the Indians attempted to steal their guns, but were caught.

Then, the party killed two Blackfoot braves, who were stealing their horses; they were the only Indians killed during their three-year journey. Drouillard swore up and down that the band was Gros Ventre. Lewis left a peace medal on the body of the warrior he shot. The party retreated by horseback and canoe to the mouth of the Marias River and the Missouri River to their rendezvous point.

The Blackfoot embraced the Hudson's Bay and other Canadian fur traders, but not on the Missouri River. The white men of the north were accepted, but not the American "Long Knives." Trappers that they met convinced Colter and Potts to get a release from the military and join them trapping. On returning to St. Louis, Congress gave each of them 320 acres of land for their service. The adventuresome Colter returned with them to the mouth of the Platte River. There he joined Manuel Lisa on a beaver hunting expedition. Potts was there; and the two continued on with Manuel Lisa down the Missouri and Yellowstone Rivers to the mouth of the Big Horn River, where they built a fort for their headquarters.

Lisa wanted the fort for the fur trade with the Indians and sent Colter out to broadcast the idea. He crossed Jackson Hole and the Tetons. Colter followed the Big Horn, Wind, Green, Snake and Yellowstone Rivers. John was one of the first white men in Yellowstone Park.

Later that summer, Colter was a reluctant participant in a war against 1,500 Blackfoot Indians. Colter had been a friend to the Crow Indians and joined the war party with 300 Crow and 500 Flathead warriors against the Blackfoot. He was injured in the battle.

Colter and Potts canoed up the Yellowstone River to trap beaver. They carried their canoe overhead across Bozeman Pass and paddled down the Gallatin River to the three forks of the Missouri River. They paddled up the westernmost fork of the Jefferson River. Remembering combat with the Blackfoot Indians earlier, Colter kept his ear to the ground. They canoed six miles on downstream. Suddenly they were surrounded by hundreds of Blackfoot warriors. They signaled for them to beach the canoe. Colter slipped their traps into the water and paddled to shore. As they touched shore, a warrior grabbed Potts' rifle from his hands and Colter immediately wrenched it from the warrior's grip.

An arrow penetrated Potts' chest. Potts shot the warrior that killed him. Several more arrows struck Potts. He slumped over dying. They held Colter down and wrestled his clothing from him. They freed Colter, and he stood there naked. The Chief motioned him away. He stood there, confused. Then he saw the warriors disrobing, taking off their blankets and deerskin garb. The Chief held his hand up. Warriors were poised for the chase with knives and war clubs. He was given a head start. When his hand dropped they would begin the chase.

Colter finally got the idea. He was about to "run the gauntlet," a game of run for your life. If Colter escaped, he was free. If they caught him, he would be tortured and killed. He thought, "run," and took off like a shot. Colter did not look back running as hard as he could. Keeping his speed, Colter exerted himself until he was winded, blood oozed from his nose. He glanced over his shoulder and saw a brave close behind him. He spun around surprising the Indian; he grabbed his spear pinning him to the ground.

Colter sped on and ran until he reached the Madison River. He dove in and surfaced beneath some floating driftwood, unseen. He remained there beneath the debris; at times, the Indians stood directly over him, searching.

Colter promised God that if he escaped alive, he would never return to Indian country. Finally, the Indians returned to camp as darkness fell. He swam downstream, waded out and started running. Colter remained on the move all night to get as far away from the Blackfeet as possible. He walked for seven days and nights to Lisa's fort, 250 miles distant. Colter arrived tired, cold, starved and naked, with a full growth of beard.

He rested for some time. Colter remembered the traps that he submerged in the river. He left to return to the Jefferson River to get those traps. Colter sat along the Gallatin River, in front of his camp fire, as arrows whizzed around him. He ran up the mountain and hid from the Indians. Again he prayed to God to save him, promising to leave Indian country.

This time, he kept his word. In April of 1810, Colter left Blackfeet country by paddling down the Missouri River. Colter married and settled down in Missouri, near the home of Daniel Boone.

Blackfoot Country included much of Canada and Montana country. It was referred to as "Fur Country," because of the number of furs traded there. For generations, Blackfoot war parties crossed and re-crossed the forty-ninth parallel dividing the countries. They had the freedom to come and go. When the Blackfoot first encountered white explorers and fur trappers, they called them "Big Knives." The famous fur traders, Andrew Henry, Manuel Lisa and Pierre Menard were driven out of the Upper Missouri River region by the Blackfoot.

At the trading posts, like Fort Belknap and Fort Benton, the Indians traded for tobacco, cloth, calico, gingham, needles, and thread. Axes, cartridges, knives, pots and frying pans were obtained there. Sugar, flour and coffee were bartered for in using pint sized cups.

In 1822, Andrew Henry built a small trading post at the mouth of the Yellowstone River. The next spring, Henry led a party of trappers up the Missouri. Near Great Falls, the party was attacked by Blackfoot Indians. Four trappers were slain before they could retreat downstream.

In 1823, Hudson's Bay trapper, Alexander Ross, erected "Flathead Post," called the "Second Salish House" or "Kullyspell House," near Sand Point, five miles from Thompson Falls, in Flathead Indian country. Ross's beaver brigade of 140 men, including Iroquois Indians, penetrated Idaho's Salmon River country reaping over 5,000 beaver skins that year and nearly depleting the beaver there. Additional brigade leaders, James W. Dease and John Work, were added in the field because of the rich trapping yields in the Snake River region. Brigade leader, John Work, traded out of Fort Nez Perce. Work became renowned as a Hudson's Bay trader working with the

Blackfoot and Salish Indians in the field. Items exchanged for furs were axes, beads, blankets, pipes, coffee, guns, knives, mirrors and tobacco.

Peter Skene Ogden replaced Ross in the field, serving from 1824-1831, for the Hudson's Bay Company as beaver brigade leader into the Snake River drainage. In 1825, Fort Vancouver was erected north of the Columbia River by veteran Chief Factor John McLoughlin of the Western District of the Hudson's Bay Company that had expanded from Canada for the fur trade. The British began to develop their interests in the Pacific Northwest.

In 1825, in what became Wyoming, the Rocky Mountain Fur Company began conducting an annual spring rendezvous. Friendly Indians and free trappers met there to sell their furs. The Fur Company conducted trade for goods transported up the Platte and Missouri Rivers, across the Rocky Mountains.

Jim Beckwourth was a mountain man and a fur trapper. He was born in Virginia, the son of a plantation owner and a mulatto slave. He was of mixed blood and faced rejection at times. In 1824, young Beckwourth signed on as a blacksmith and a servant with a fur trading expedition into the Rocky Mountains. He stayed on as a fur trapper in the mountains. Jim Beckwourth was one of the few black mountain men. Beckwourth lived with the Blackfoot Indians, the most feared Indian tribe on the Plains. He married the daughter of a chief.

The Blackfoot scalped three fur trappers and returned to camp with the scalp locks and prepared for a scalp dance. Beckwourth forbid his wife to participate in the dance. She defied him and danced anyway. Beckwourth walked up and cold cocked her with a tomahawk. The Indians grabbed him, ready to kill the black man, when the girl's father stopped them and stood up for him, saying that the girl disobeyed her husband.

Beckwourth was given another daughter of the chief for a wife. That night, the wounded bride sought forgiveness and he took both wives. That coming spring, he sold thirty-five bales of beaver pelts to William Ashley, and sent the Indians back to camp with blankets and trinkets.

Beckwourth returned to St. Louis and looked for Eliza, his true love. She had not waited, but married someone else. Beckwourth returned to the mountains and married a Crow woman, around 1830. He left the village and traveled to the southwest, where he married a Spanish wife, but she ran off. He again returned to live with the Crow Indians and lived with them for many years, became a warrior, hunted buffalo and went on raids for horses.

Jim Beckwourth was a teller of tall tales. The stories that he told his biographer were a bit too exaggerated to be completely true. Jim led a life of adventure, but how much? Jim told this yarn about a pretty Crow princess, named Red Cherry.

She was the most beautiful woman in the whole Crow village and had a husband, Chief Big Rain. Many men in the village desired her. Beckwourth went directly to Big Rain's lodge. She asked him what he wanted. "I have come here because I love you," he said. "Don't you realize that I belong to the chief?" "Yes, but he doesn't love you like I do. He does not go to war. I will paint your face and bring you horses. As long as you are Big Rain's, he won't paint your face." She said, "Big Rain will kill you."

Jim Beckwourth left Red Cherry's teepee with her ring on his finger. The following day, he led a raid against the Blackfoot. When he returned, Jim sent her a message. "We will elope tonight. Where shall I meet you?" They elected to honeymoon while on a Blackfoot raid. Big Rain was angry when they returned with many horses and found his wife missing.

Big Rain and his six sisters severely beat Jim upon his return. Jim fell to the ground, during the beating. Had he resisted, they would have been justified in killing him. By their rule, had they drawn blood on him, he could have killed them. One of Jim's wives scolded him for taking Big Rain's wife, when he could easily have more. Beckwourth maintained that he had only wanted the most beautiful woman in his lodge.

Jim celebrated with a horse dance before joining the raiding party to count coup on the Blackfeet. Big Cherry strolled out of her lodge and joined them. Four days later, they returned with a victory and counted three scalps. Big Rain and his sisters again flogged Beckwourth. He was greeted in his lodge by his wife and new baby boy. She said he would be like his father.

Two nights after his reprimand, Jim, Red Cherry and many warriors went on another raid to steal Blackfoot horses. When he returned, Jim was again beaten. This time some warriors that followed Beckwourth confronted Big Rain. "You have flogged him three times now. And you will beat him no more. Red Cherry loves him and she does not love you. You could turn the Bighorn River uphill, but you could not separate them."

"We will buy your right to her and give her to Red Arm (Jim Beckwourth). As a great chief, you would hate to want a woman who loves a warrior more than you." But Big Rain still loved her. He released her for one war horse, 10 guns, 10 chief's coats, scarlet cloth, 10 pairs of new leggings, and 10 pairs of new moccasins. Jim had a new bride in his lodge.

Beckwourth took more than one Crow bride and had several children. He finally attained the position of head chief. In 1855, one of his sons became chief of the entire Crow Nation.

While visiting a Crow village in Montana in 1866, Jim Beckwourth died. The Crow interred him in a tree platform, in Indian tradition. He had been chief of the Crow. He fought in the Seminole Wars and was in California during the Gold Rush. He also served as an Army scout for Colonel Chivington in the Sand Creek Massacre.

If one asked a Blackfoot warrior his name, he would not disclose it. Speaking one's own name in public was unlucky in life, according to their superstition. This could have been why so few names of Blackfeet chiefs are known. A warrior changed his name, nearly every time he counted coup in battle, since he was entitled then to do so.

There were three strong tribes of the Plains Indians. They were the Blackfoot of the Northwest, the Comanche-Kiowa of the Southern Plains and the Sioux of the Northern Plains.

When Prince Maximilian visited the Crow Indians in the 1830's, he was amazed at the number of horses they possessed. A village of 400 teepees owned 10,000 horses. They were made rich from horses raids. He was also impressed by their bows, wrapped in rattlesnake skins. He was invited to sleep in the chief's lodge. The prince slept undisturbed in the lodge with the chief's whole family.

Maximilian described the Blackfoot males as muscular and some women and girls as being quite pretty. The men were broad shouldered, stocky built and of medium height.

In 1832, Indian artist George Catlin visited the Blackfoot Indians. He commented that the Blackfoot Confederation was "the most powerful tribe of Indians on the continent." He estimated their population at 16,500. That year, Catlin met a free trapper at Fort Union, who had made seven expeditions. The trapper was robbed five times by Blackfoot Indians of his equipment, furs and horses; lucky to be alive, the man was ready to give up.

Washakie was a famous tribal leader of the Eastern Shoshoni Indians in what became Wyoming Territory. He lived from 1804-1900. The mother of Washakie was a Lemhi Shoshoni. Washakie was first called *Pinaquana* or "sweet smelling," in the Shoshoni tongue. Sacajawea visited her people about the same time that he was born.

His father was killed during a Blackfoot raid on their village when he was very young. His mother escaped with her five children at that time and joined her Shoshoni people. He lived with the Shoshoni for about five years before conjoining with the Bannock Indians. He grew to become a man and killed his first buffalo, skinned it and cured the hide. From the hide, he cut a piece of leather and made a rattle with pebbles inside. Washakie earned his name pronounced, *Was-sik-he*. Washakie, means "gourd rattle," in the Shoshonean tongue. He rode among Blackfoot, Crow and Sioux, with much bravery, and scared their horses with his rattle; in fear of a rattlesnake, they bucked, reared, or bolted, sometimes throwing the rider.

Around 20 years of age, Washakie transferred his allegiance to the Eastern Shoshonis. Soon after, a raiding war party of Blackfoot Indians rode in and took many of their horses, counting coup. Washakie assembled a war party and pursued the Blackfoot warriors north. They tracked the marauders for nearly 600 miles. His party retrieved the stolen horses, but brought back many enemy scalps. In the next encounter with them, Washakie did not fare as well; a Blackfoot arrow struck him just below his left eye, leaving a scar.

Three hundred Shoshoni warriors arrived at the 1837 Rendezvous, led by Chief Washakie. Jesuit Father, Pierre Jean De Smet, was present.

In the late 1850's, Washakie led a Shoshoni war party against the Crow Indians. The fighting went on for three days and finally fought to a standstill. At that point, Chief Washakie and Crow Chief Big Robber faced off for a duel. Washakie killed the chief, cut out his heart and ate it raw, as the Crows watched. The Crow Indians never attacked the Shoshoni again.

The oral history of the tribe relates that Washakie wanted hymns sung in the Shoshoni tongue. He urged his people to continue their beadwork in the old ways in color and design, so that the traditions of their ancient ones would not be forgotten.

The chief was successful in war. He was a very famous chief, esteemed by many. Washakie was awarded the coveted peace medal among Indians, by President Andrew Johnson in 1866. The peace medal was awarded by 20 Presidents to peaceable Indian chiefs.

When his young braves wanted to go on raids, he told them to go to the graves of the ones that died on the war path and see his reasons for peace. Washakie fought the government, who wanted to take the Shoshoni's hunting rights and have them farm instead. He patrolled to keep Indian war parties from attacking settlers. The chief signed the Treaty of Fort Laramie and the Treaty of Fort Bridger. He was close friends with his son-in-law, Jim Bridger, and Kit Carson. A fort in Wyoming was named Fort Washakie, in his honor.

The chief was friend to the pioneer, fur trapper and the U.S. Army. Chief Washakie's enemies were the Teton Sioux. He joined the Army against the warring Sioux, who had killed his son. Washakie scouted for the U.S. Army under General Crook. Washakie received a silver saddle from President Grant and a peace medal from President Andrew Johnson.

When Washakie was over 70 years of age, the young tribesmen said that they needed a younger chief, who could count coup and take scalps. The old chief disappeared for nearly two months. When he rode into camp, there were six fresh scalps hanging from his belt.

Washakie lived to the ripe old age of about 100 years. He became a Christian three years before his death, joining the Episcopalian Church. Washakie was blind and in ill health when he died in 1900. He was buried with full military honors at Fort Washakie in his beloved Wind River Mountains of Wyoming. Chief Washakie is the only Native American in that era to receive a full military funeral.

Throughout his life, Chief Washakie was a visionary. Planning on a rich life in heaven, he dreamed of beautiful Indian women around him. There were many horses and pure mountain streams, plenty of fish and meat so plentiful that his people would never go hungry.

The Great Treaty Council of 1868 established the Wind River Reservation. After that, all reservations were created by executive order. The reserve set aside for Washakie's Shoshoni people was the Wind River Reservation in central Wyoming. The reserve is home to both the Eastern Shoshoni and the Northern Arapaho, with 2,650 Shoshoni members. The reservation covers 2,268,008 acres. The Arapaho were called the "Blue Sky People," by other tribes, because they were a mild mannered people.

Christopher Houston Carson was nicknamed "Kit." He was one of America's most famous mountain men and Indian fighters. Raised in Missouri, Carson went to Taos, where he made his home. Carson trapped for furs in the Rockies for years with men like Jim Bridger, Thomas Fitzpatrick, and Joe Meek, also trapped for a short time for the Hudson's Bay Company. Carson lived around Indians, learning their customs and languages. He served as an Army scout and an Indian fighter; he fought the Arapaho, Blackfeet, Comanche, Kiowa, and Navajo.

Chief Washakie's daughter married Jim Bridger. Bridger was an Indian fighter, who fought the Blackfoot, who were fierce foes. He spoke Bannock, Shoshoni and other Indian dialects, besides Indian sign language. He even knew some French and Spanish.

#40. Washakie, Chief of the Wind and Green River Shoshoni People
(Photograph Cowtesy of Azusa Publishing, LLC)

134

Legend does not tell us that Jim Bridger was a prevaricator. It is possible that the story was told and retold so many times that the yarn was embellished to sound better. Jim Bridger, along with four partners, purchased the Rocky Mountain Fur Company in 1830. They moved the operation to the upper Missouri River in Blackfoot Country, because of strong competition.

The Blackfoot disliked Jim trapping animals in Blackfoot country. Bridger led a party of trappers and ran into a war party of Blood Indians. Bridger rode ahead to council the war chief; he extended his hand in friendship. The chief grabbed Bridger's rifle instead, as two arrows penetrated Jim's back. The mountain man reined his horse, turned and raced back to the trappers, in a shower of arrows. A short skirmish occurred before the warriors disappeared.

The trappers removed the arrows; but one arrowhead remained, lodged in his backbone. Three years later, at the Green River rendezvous, Doctor Marcus Whitman removed the arrowhead with a butcher knife for a scalpel and no anesthetic, as Jim gritted his teeth.

Another version of Jim and the Blackfoot goes like this. One morning, a small band of angry Blackfoot Indians was in hot pursuit of Jim Bridger. Bridger hightailed it. His horse was in a full gallop. He headed for the fort. His mount became lathered and exhausted. Jim rode for his life and managed to stay alive.

He kept his scalp, but caught an arrow in the back. Jim survived three years with the arrow-head stuck in his backbone. Finally, Reverend Markus Whitman removed the arrow, without anesthetic. Both stories end the same and may be another version of the same yarn.

A law was passed in 1834, prohibiting the sale of alcohol to the Indians, but that did not stop whiskey runners from selling illegal liquor. Forts that illegally dispensed "moon-shine," to the Indians soon became known as "whiskey forts." These illegal forts were established in the interior during this time. The Blackfoot Indians procured the "white lightning," there. Indians referred to alcohol as "the white man's water."

#41. Chief Washakie and His Shoshoni Village
(Photograph Courtesy of Azusa Publishing, LLC)

Born around 1800, Rotten Belly was a great leader of the Crow Nation. A war chief, Rotten Belly succeeded *Arapooish*, who was called the greatest Crow Chief. They called Rotten Belly a holy man and a prophet, a kind of medicine man. He acted on his instincts, sometimes endangering his own safety. Rotten Belly was a quiet man.

As a young chief, Rotten Belly led 400 warriors on the war path against the Blackfoot Indians. Crow spies had watched their village for days before the raid. Rotten Belly assembled his warriors at night in order to make the attack at dawn. The war party caught them off guard. The Blackfoot were outnumbered and suffered a heavy loss. The Blackfoot counted 100 dead; the Crow party lost only 22 warriors.

Years earlier, a Cheyenne war party massacred a band of 30 Crow lodges. When Rotten Belly returned from visiting the Flathead Indians, he led six hundred warriors on the war trail. They caught the Cheyenne near the Arkansas River. The enemy encampment was between two creeks. Moving by cover of darkness, the Crows surrounded the sleeping camp.

At daybreak, they stampeded the Cheyenne's horses. They were ambushed by the Crows. Surrounded, they had no avenue of escape. As the fighting slowed to a standstill, two hundred Cheyenne lay dead. They left no survivors. Rotten Belly took over 300 women and children captive and over 1,000 horses. The Crow lost only five men with one dozen wounded.

On the trek home, the Crow warriors contracted smallpox, caught apparently from immigrants or the captives, and brought the dreaded disease home to their village; one out of six lived through the epidemic. Most escaped to the mountains.

At that time, Chief Rotten Belly took measures to preserve his band. He sent runners out in all directions to round up any surviving members of the tribe. Rotten Belly reorganized the remaining families, finding husbands and wives for those that were single, using the Cheyenne captives. He distributed horses, rifles, provisions among the surviving tribe's people.

Chief Rotten Belly had saved his dying band. He decided to raid a fur fort in Blackfoot Country and would attack the white eyes that had given them smallpox, in retaliation. They planned to capture guns, ammunition and horses. The Blackfoot Indians had migrated north to barter at the trading posts. The Crow marauders looked for no serious confrontation. The Crows attacked the fur fort. The fur trappers held them off for nearly a month. The warriors attacked, but could not capture the fort.

Rotten Belly had said previously that if they could not capture the fort he would leave his body in the Land of the Blackfoot Indians. As the Blackfoot Indians returned, Rotten Belly took his own life. The Crow Tribe returned to the mountains. Tales of the deeds of Rotten Belly lived on. That was the last time they followed the war trail.

Before the smallpox epidemic of 1837, the Blackfoot numbered 150 lodges. Nearly half of the Small Robe Band survived the plague. Smallpox and measles killed 6,000 Blackfoot Indians in 1837. The smallpox epidemic overall killed half of their tribe. The devastation caused by the white man was overpowering for the Blackfoot.

Their hunting ground was Three Forks, south of the Missouri River, the same country where the Flathead tribe came to hunt the buffalo. It was very unusual, but the Small Robe Blackfoot Indians made peace with the Flatheads, a Piegan enemy. The Small Robes hunted with the Flathead and traded with them.

The Small Robes observed their brother Flatheads in awe when they saw them praying and crossing themselves. An old Iroquois Indian and his party had migrated from the north to their village. The old Indian, Ignace Lamoose, converted to Catholicism in Montreal at a Jesuit mission, there. He taught them Catholic prayers and to observe the Sabbath Day.

In 1835, Ignace and his two sons went back to St. Louis and the old Iroquois urged them to send a delegation to St. Louis to ask for a missionary, but none was sent. Two years later, Ignace and a party of four made the trip. Along the way, they were all killed by a Sioux Indian war party, possibly mistaking them for Shoshoni Indians. Two years passed and Peter Left-hand and young Ignace traveled with friendly traders back east. Their trip was a success as they were promised a missionary the following spring.

The two accompanied Father Pierre Jean De Smet, the Catholic missionary of the Jesuit order, across the plains and mountains in the spring of 1840. Encouraged, Father De Smet met with the Flatheads before returning to St. Louis. In the autumn of 1841, Father De Smet returned to the Flathead people, bringing two Jesuit priests and two lay brothers. At the initial Flathead mission, the first Blackfoot was converted to Christianity with four of his family. He received the Christian name, Nicholas. Twenty Small Robes, with Nicholas, took instruction at the Flathead Mission. The Indians found Christianity to be powerful "war medicine."

#42. Father De Smet
Author Photo

In 1840, Father De Smet came to live among the Blackfoot Indians. They called the Jesuit missionaries "Black Robes," terminology for the missionaries because of their vesture. They called Father De Smet, "*Innu-e-kinni*" (Long Teeth, in the Blackfoot tongue). It is possible that the priest's teeth were normal, but the Blackfoot peoples' teeth were ground down from a lifetime of eating food ground in stone mortars.

Father De Smet lived in a lodge in the center of the Blackfoot camp. A bell was rung to apprise the Indians of impending services. He remained with these Indians a long time christening and baptizing them. Father De Smet would take the hunters and their families to the tent of worship and implore them to kneel and pray to the Great Spirit and thank Him for the hunt and the safe return. On the Sabbath, the priest held mass from morning until noon and expected them to attend. Three Blackfoot clans accepted Christianity. Father De Smet returned to the Flathead Indians. He sent two other Black Robe priests to the Blackfoot. One priest remained there, and the other went on to serve the Gros Ventre Indian people.

In autumn, Father De Smet had the opportunity to hold a peace council between the Blackfoot and Flathead Indians. Peace seemed to be decided. It was in early autumn of 1846 when Chief Victor prepared to go on a buffalo hunt and invited the Small Robes to join them. Twelve lodges of Small Robes joined his party. While on the hunt, the Small Robes were ambushed by the powerful Crow Indians. Most all of the males were killed. The fierce Crow took nearly 200 women and children captive. The massacre nearly wiped out the Small Robes population. Later, 50 captives were released to go back to their camp. Only a few remained. The Small Robes Tribe was later completely annihilated by smallpox.

In 1846, the Oregon Treaty was signed between Great Britain and the United States. The Treaty established the 49th Parallel and gave America Fort Vancouver, Fort Walla-Walla, Colville, Nasqually and Okanogan, that had been the possession of the Hudson's Bay Company, for the asking price of $2,000,000. America responded with one-tenth that amount as fair value.

In the summer of 1847, the Small Robes again joined the Flatheads on a buffalo hunt. Again they were attacked by the powerful Crow Indians, but this time the Small Robes, as revenge for the deaths of their brothers, fought valiantly, pushing back the Crow invaders in victory. The Small Robes attributed the prayers of their ally, Flatheads,' prayers to their victory.

The Blackfoot and Flathead Indians had been in a continual state of war. Father De Smet arranged a peace council in the autumn among the

Blackfoot Indians and the Flatheads. The council was a success. The Small Robes begged Father De Smet to baptize them and their children. September 15, 1847, he held mass where 2,000 lodges assembled, including the Blood, Flatheads, Gros Ventre of the Plains, Nez Perce from west of the Rockies, Northern Blackfoot and Piegan were camped. The next day, the priest had translated prayers into their dialect. *God Almighty. Piegan are His children. He is going to help us on earth; if you are good, He will save your soul.*

The priest learned from a Blood Indian leader that 60 Northern Blackfoot children had been baptized by Father Thibault, from Red River, invited by John Rowland, chief factor of the Hudson's Bay Company to serve the Indians. Most all of them wore crosses from their necks.

Confident that he had made peace between the two tribes, Father De Smet returned to the east. In his stead, the priest left Father Nicholas Point to administer to the Blackfoot Indians. The French priest was a gifted artist and a devout Jesuit. He headquartered at Fort Lewis, the Post of the American Fur Company on the Missouri. The priest baptized twenty-two children before preaching to the Blackfoot hunting camps for several weeks.

Father Point's portraits won over several chief's friendship. The Blackfoot looked at him as a "medicine man." They thought that he could heal and do magic.

Adult Indians did not want to give up their old religion. Father Point chastised them for having more than one wife and for their constant warfare. They did not want to give up polygamy for Christianity or elect to quit raiding enemy camps for horses and scalps. The warriors let him baptize them; if they could be made invincible to their enemies.

Father Point had prayers translated into the Blackfoot tongue and was a witness of Christ. The priest conducted classes in Christian doctrine for men, women, and children. Point was in contact with Father De Smet by mail. He told him that progress with the Blackfoot was slow. He related to him that they would not let go of their old ways and accept Christianity.

The priest left his post at Fort Lewis on May 19, 1847 by barge. It would be twelve years until the Black Robes returned to the Blackfoot Indians to build a substantial Jesuit mission. Blackfoot Indians would again have their "medicine men" in Black Robes.

Meanwhile, they went back to their old ways of raiding the Flathead Indians. Polk appointed a Governor to Oregon Territory and two military companies to Fort Vancouver, on March 2, 1849 and assigned an Army Regiment to the Northwest for duty.

In 1850 St. Mary's Jesuit Mission was forced to close due to numerous raids by Blackfoot marauders. A Blackfoot Indian raid on Saint Mary's caused such fear in the community that the clergy in charge was forced to shut the mission down. The Kalispel traded horses and canoes to Major John Owen, the trader who had purchased the old St. Mary's mission.

St. Ignatius was having problems, also. They quit farming and returned to the old way of hunting and digging roots to live. They traded for guns and continued warring and stealing horses. The next year, Fort Sarpy was abandoned by the American Fur Company due to Blackfoot attacks.

The Blackfoot fought the Assiniboine, Bannock, Crow, Flathead, Shoshoni and Sioux, but never fought the United States Army. Actually, they were at war, but it was never declared.

The Cheyenne and Sarsi were allies, as were the Atsina, Hidatsa (a variant tribe of Crow). The Atsina called themselves the "Clay People" and are related to the Arapaho. The French named them the Gros Ventre or the "Big Belly" Tribe. The Blackfoot called them the "Gut People." There was intermarriage between them.

In 1853, Blackfoot and Atsina warriors fought over the death of two Gros Ventre braves. The two tribes were old allies. The Blackfoot took prisoners and treated them well. They were fed, given horses and freed. Their actions led to a treaty between the tribes two years later.

There were fairly good relations for a time between the Indians and the traders. Traders were free to roam in Blackfoot Country and were welcomed in their camps. The Blackfoot traded with the Hudson's Bay Company on the Saskatchewan in Canada and on the Upper Missouri.

Some of the Blackfoot tribe crossed the border into Canada prior to the treaty. The majority of the Blackfoot and Piegan were at peace. It was the Bloods who were riled up. There were no troops to protect the whites. There were plenty of lawless white men and Indians, for that matter. White vigilante groups were formed to protect the people.

Hudson's Bay traders were suspected of trading ball and powder to the Blackfoot Indians in exchange for stolen horses at Rocky Mountain House, near Fort Benton. However, they did hold back the percussion caps in trade for their own protection. An Indian could fire six to ten arrows before a white man could reload his muzzle-loader.

#43. Nez Perce Woman
(Photograph Courtesy of Azusa Publishing, LLC)

The Blackfoot were nearly obliterated by smallpox by 1835. The Northern Blackfoot Indian League of Canada and the Southern Piegan of the Northern Plains were one of the larger Indian Confederations. The term, Blackfoot is used for these Indians in Canada. The Blackfoot Sioux are no relation to the Blackfoot Indians.

The *Kainai* tribe is also called the "Blood Blackfoot." There are two stories from legend that tell us why the tribe was named "Blood." Long ago Blackfoot warriors returned to camp after a raid on the Kutenai; their hands and faces were covered with blood from scalping. Another story told of the first traders that saw the Kainai and their ceremonial objects covered with sacred ochre (red iron dust) and called them the "red people."

A Blackfoot stranger came to their village and asked who their chief was? Everyone answered, "I am." The Blackfoot spoke and said, "I will call you the tribe of many chiefs." The tribal name "Kainai" also means "many chiefs."

# Chapter Ten
## Treaties and Reservations

The Blackfoot Council on October 16, 1855, was conducted at the mouth of the Judith River by Governor Stevens. A peace treaty was written and signed by the Blackfoot, Flathead, Gros Ventre, Kutenai, Nez Perce, and Pend d' Oreille tribes. The Lame Bull Treaty of 1855 was signed by Blood Chief Medicine Calf and Calf Shirt. Calf Shirt was sub-chief and Running Wolf was their spiritual leader.

The treaty created shared buffalo hunting in Blackfoot territory, east of the Rockies. These tribes agreed not to make war against any other tribe, except in self-defense. A common hunting ground was agreed on between the Mussel-Shell River and Yellowstone. All tribes could have access.

Establishing an Indian school in 1855 resulted in literacy. By 1884, sixteen Blackfoot Indians were able to read English.

The white man could go anywhere unharmed. The government could construct roads through any part of the country. The government agreed to pay the Blackfoot $20,000 annually for ten years and a further sum of $15,000 per year for 15 years. In addition, they would receive instruction in agricultural pursuits and in educating their children. The Treaty strictly enforced peace with the whites, but they were allowed to continue warring against the Assiniboine and Crow Indians.

In 1860, the Blackfoot were pronounced the most passive tribe on the Missouri River. Their annuities were brought up river by boat each year and dispersed to them. Farming was unsuccessful. It was too dry and they had no irrigation. There were no schools or missions at this time. There was fighting among the tribes.

They must have had a double standard. The Blackfoot raided white settlements in Montana, in the 1860's. The Indian war parties were made up of the Blood, Northern Blackfoot and Piegan tribesmen. It makes sense that boot-leg whiskey was a factor in fueling the Blackfoot to go on raids. The Blackfoot drove the stolen horses across the border to safety.

In 1861, a Pend d' Oreille band from west of the Rockies had stolen horses from the Gros Ventre, allies of the Blackfoot. They abandoned the horses near a Piegan camp. The Gros Ventre discovered their horses and lost no time attacking the Piegan camp. The Piegan warriors retaliated by raiding the Gros Ventre in small sallies, stealing their horses. In the meantime, the Gros Ventre made a peace pact with the River Crow Indians.

The Gold Rush of 1862 in Blackfoot Country seemed to upset the world of the traditional Blackfoot people. During a short period of time, 15,000 miners came to occupy their land. They mined for gold in Indian Territory. Their hunting grounds were overrun. The buffalo were dying off. The beaver trapped out. Their old life style was disappearing, along with their dreams and yet, no war broke out. With the white men came disease. In 1864, 1,000 Blackfoot Indians died of scarlet fever.

In 1863, a large sum of money was paid by the United States government to the Hudson's Bay Company for the Province of Oregon. Then, in 1868, Britain relinquished rights to the monopoly over Rupert's Land. The Hudson's Bay Company was the first business venture in the Pacific Northwest and the only kind of rule in the beginning. It laid the foundation for the United States government to step in.

Though the older tribe members were peaceable, young reckless braves wanted to raid, count coup and steal horses. In December of 1864, a party of Blood Indians stole horses from twenty trappers. Nine trappers followed and overtook them. They killed two and retrieved their horses. Bad feelings arose in the Blood tribe after that.

Also in 1864, war broke out with the Sioux over roads constructed in their region. The Blackfoot volunteered to help fight their old enemies, the Sioux Nation.

Some Blood Blackfeet stole forty horses from the white men at Fort Benton on April 23, 1865. A month later, a party of Blood Indians visited Fort Benton. They were attacked by white men and three Blood warriors were killed.

Two days later, Chief Calf Shirt (who had signed the 1855 Treaty) and a large party of Blood Indians came upon ten woodcutters at the mouth of the Marias River, twelve miles from Fort Benton. The party of Indians killed all of them. Their bodies were discovered and Governor Edgerton, fearing war with the Blackfoot, sent James Stuart and a party of volunteers to punish the band of warriors. They found that the Blood band had ridden north into Canada and called off their pursuit. In 1865, the Blackfeet continued to raid. The Blackfeet were feared, not only by their Amerind enemies, but also the white man.

On May 10, 1865, a war party of braves stole all of the horses and mules from a Sun River farm. Then, twelve days later, May 22, 1865, a party of drunken Bloods killed ten white men who were cutting logs on the Marias River, twelve miles from the fort.

#44. Piegan's Council
(Photograph Courtesy of Azusa Publishing, LLC)

147

The same year, a wealthy Piegan chief named Many Horses was generous to the poor. His tribe of many bands camped in the Cypress Mountains. Many Horses left the camp, accompanied by his wife to go and hunt the buffalo. During his absence, the Gros Ventre and their Crow allies made war on the Piegan camp.

The Piegan had been forewarned and were prepared to fight. During severe fighting, they learned of Chief Many Horses' death. The Piegan attacked with such ferocity that the enemy retreated. The Piegan followed and killed all that they could. Only those retreating into a stand of timber lived. Combined losses of the Crow and Gros Ventre reached 300. The Piegan only lost 20 warriors. In addition, the Piegan took captives of women and children. They also captured many horses, guns, bows, arrows and lances.

In 1865, a few tribal leaders agreed to sell their lands south of the Missouri River to the government. 2,000 square miles sold for $1,000,000. Although the treaty was never ratified, with the assent of the Indians, land was set aside for a reserve by the Executive Order of 1873. The reservation was set aside for the Blackfoot, Bloods, Gros Ventre, Piegan and River Crow Indians. The Great Northern Reservation was defined by the Act of Congress in 1874. It had first been defined in the Treaty of 1855; in part, the territory assigned to the Blackfoot in the beginning, the government had moved the southern boundary of the reservation 200 miles to the north, without compensating the Indians.

In January of 1866, two white men, accompanied by Gros Ventre Indians, were killed by a Piegan war party. Horse theft, inter-tribal war and an absence of troops made the white people uneasy.

The Blackfoot were fighting the white people and also making raids on their ranches for horses. Attempts for a treaty had failed. In 1866, Camp Cooke was established at the mouth of the Judith River, manned by one battalion of Infantry. The following year, Fort Shaw was built in the Sun River Valley. Four hundred soldiers were housed there.

Four warriors had made a friendly visit to the home of a John Morgan, who lived on Sun River. They were mistaken for warring Piegan and one of them was shot and killed. In April, 1866, a large revenge party of Piegan warriors, led by Chief Bull's Head, raided the same farm. They burned buildings and killed two workers. A new Indian agent, George Wright, visited the farm in September of 1866 to survey the damage and found it in desolation. The farm had been an experiment to demonstrate raising crops to the Blackfoot and now had failed.

Jesuit missionaries made a mistake when they took Morgan into the mission, giving him shelter. The Piegan were unforgiving and shot several cows owned by the mission and killed a herder. The mission was abandoned on April 27, 1866 and the priests found refuge. War had broken out with the Blackfoot.

One Blackfeet Indian, named Little Dog, continued to farm. In 1866, he brought twelve horses, stolen by the Piegan, to Fort Benton and turned them over to the Indian agent. When Little Dog and his family left the fort, they were overtaken by a party of drunken Piegan warriors. The Piegan killed Little Dog and his son.

*Siksikakoan,* a Blackfoot scout, rode with Major Reno under General George Armstrong Custer in 1866. There were white scouts, too, like Buffalo Bill Cody, Jim Bridger and Kit Carson.

In April of 1867, a small war party of Blackfoot Indians killed a well-known trailblazer and pioneer settler, John Bozeman, in the Yellowstone Valley. The winter of 1868, several ranchers were killed by the Blackfoot. Forts established in Blackfoot Country only antagonized them. Blackfoot Indians were angered by the nonpayment of annuities from their last treaty.

The Blackfoot fought the combined forces of the Cree and Crow Indians in the Cypress Mountain in southern Canada in 1867. The Blackfoot were victorious, killing 450 of the enemy.

The Great Treaty Council of 1868 for the purpose of establishing a reservation was signed by the Indians. After that, all reservations were created by executive order. Chief Calf Shirt signed the Treaty of 1868, as Chief of the Blood Tribe, but the treaty was never ratified.

A freight train was attacked by Indians on Eagle Creek in 1869. A driver and twenty oxen had been killed by the time that the Indians were driven off. Four warriors were killed.

There was a fracas among Indians and whites involved in a family quarrel on August 17, 1869, between Malcolm Clarke, married to a Piegan woman, their son and nephew. Clark and Bear's Head were killed. Twenty some Piegan were present. Pal, the son of Mountain Chief, shot one of Clarke's sons. Clarke's son and daughter managed to escape and survive. After reports of Clarke's death, General Sully telegraphed that he feared that the Blackfoot were in a state of war.

149

In the settlement near Silver City, in September 1869, James Quail was murdered. Some said that he was scalped by Piegan. Others said he had a gold watch and a lot of money on his person and that he was robbed by white men. Early autumn of the same year, two stage coaches were robbed. It was learned that the attack was white road bandits.

Also that autumn, the hostile Piegan had moved north and others east to Yellowstone. Horse theft subsided. The peaceable Piegan remained on the Marias River. Ten hostile Piegan returned from Yellowstone in December. Shortly thereafter, ten hunters were attacked near the head of the Sun river Valley. A government contractor and a woodcutter lost thirty mules. The thieves drove the mules over the border.

On the 13th of January, General Sully suggested capturing Mountain Chief with one half dozen warriors to solve the matter. To recover the mules, the camps of Mountain Chief, Bear Chief and Red Horn were targeted. The friendly camps of Heavy Runner, Big Leg, Little Wolf and the Boy were not bothered. Colonel E.M. Baker and four companies of cavalry from Fort Ellis were backed by two companies of mounted infantry from Fort Shaw. They left Fort Shaw on the 19th of January, 1870, arriving at the camp of Bear Chief and Red Horn at 8:00 a.m. in the morning on the 23rd.

The U.S. Army was looking for the militant band of Mountain Chief; instead, they massacred 200 from a peaceable band of Blackfoot Indians, under Chief Heavy Runner on January 23, 1870. The number of militia men was much overkill for the sleepy Indian camp of men, women and children. Out of 300 Indians, 173 were massacred, including Red Horn. Nine warriors escaped into the woods. The rest were killed or captured, mostly women and children.

The Blood tribe protested, saying that the Indians killed were primarily women and children and there was smallpox in the camp. The Army defended its actions and claimed it was like any routine maneuver.

The Army deduced that 173 Indians were too many to have been killed from only 37 lodges. Having been the senior officer in charge of the attack, General Sheridan stated that neither he nor any other officer advocated killing women and children, although he justified the attack.

General Sheridan responded with these words:"If the lives and property of citizens of Montana can best be protected by striking the Indians, I want them struck. Tell Baker to strike them hard." The newspapers back East responded. One editorial blamed the army and sided with the Indians over the massacre.

#45. Cheyenne Maiden & Doll
(Photograph Courtesy of Azusa Publishing, LLC)

151

Traders Healy and Hamilton introduced "repeating rifles," to the Blackfeet. The Blood and the Piegan's teepees were pitched on the Oldman and St. Mary's Rivers in the autumn of 1870 for trade at the whiskey forts.

At daybreak a large war party of Assiniboine and Cree Indians attacked the Bloods while they were under the influence of whiskey. Hearing dogs barking and gunfire, the neighboring Piegan mounted up and joined the melee. The combined Blackfoot drove the enemy into the river and made short work of them with their repeating rifles.

The Blackfoot had forced the Assiniboine and Cree enemies into retreat. Rifles were used in hunting and warfare, replacing the bow and arrow. The weapons could be loaded while on horseback; the repeating rifles revolutionized buffalo hunting and improved warfare. The battle with the Cree was the last great battle fought by the Blackfoot.

On October 6, 1870, General De Trobiand remarked that there was no Indian war in the territory, but just a few unruly Indians. His idea was that those hostiles be brought into custody. General Sheridan agreed and pointed out that Mountain Chief was the worst offender.

Ranchers were losing horses and some lost their lives. The Army and the local authorities did not pursue them into Canada, as long as they crossed what was called the "medicine line" or the forty-ninth parallel. The Blackfoot knew no borders. Certain American traders crossed the border into Canada to trade pistols, rifles, and ammunition to the Blackfoot. The Indians, on the other hand, returned to Rocky Mountain House with a revolver in their belts, endangering the trader's lives.

Canadian traders opened "whiskey forts" and introduced the Indians to the deadly alcohol; one of many, who suffered from alcohol, was Blood Chief, Calf Shirt, who could not hold his liquor and was mean spirited after drinking. These traders feared him and gave him too much whiskey in trade for the head-to-tail buffalo robes. Sometimes he came for whiskey with no trade, but they would appease him with a gallon of hooch. He begged whiskey so often that the traders grew tired of him and planned his demise.

One whiskey such fort was Fort Hoop Up. In 1870, during the traders' absence, Indians burned the fort to the ground. It was later rebuilt on a grandiose scale. The lure of alcohol brought many Blackfeet to the forts with horses, furs, buffalo robes and even women in trade for whiskey.

When Blood Chief, Calf Shirt again came to Joe Kipp's fort asking for whiskey, he was given poisoned firewater instead. He took a drink and said that the booze was bad, but drank it anyway. He came back to the fort late that night asking for whiskey. He was given more whiskey, with stronger poison, but was not affected and again asked for more whiskey. They failed and then told him to go home. He asked for more whiskey.

Angry, the renegade traders produced their guns and fired at the chief. Calf Shirt's spirit power came from the bear. Bullets could not hurt him; they tried to tie him up, but did not succeed. He fought them off and walked out of the store. It was winter as they shot at him, hit him with an axe, and finally put a lynch rope around his neck and dragged him to the pond into the water. They used long poles to hold him below the water. In the morning they returned and cut the rope, and never saw Calf Shirt again.

Alcohol proved to be a curse to the Indians. In the 1870's, many Blackfoot died due to the dreaded liquor. The Montana Indian agent estimated that 600 barrels of whiskey were sold to the Indians in 1873. Montana Indian Agent, George Wright, had some whiskey runners arrested. Liquor was the cause of death for 25% of the Blackfoot tribe. They died from alcohol poisoning, homicides in drunken brawls, or freezing to death after a night of drinking. The government attempted to prevent the Blackfoot Indians from obtaining firewater by limiting their trading to just two legal posts. It was ironic that the Blackfoot contracted the white man's smallpox and the rot-gut poison alcohol in close proximity.

In 1877, the Blackfeet Indians signed Treaty #7 and settled onto reservations in southern Alberta. At the time of their treaties, the Blackfeet camped east of Calgary. The Bloods resided to the south on the Belly, Oldman and St. Mary's Rivers. The southern Piegan lodged along the upper Missouri River drainage. The Blackfoot have expanded southward.

On the reservation, the Blackfeet suffered from starvation and disease. More died than were born. The Piegan were robbed of their own ration and allocations by their agents. The mighty Blackfoot Indians were now stripped of their power; without the buffalo they were forced to survive on government rations. Some starved. They received too few supplies and very little money due to crooked Indian agents. Congress was to blame.

From 1871-1878, Congress cut their allocations from $50,000 annually to $40,000, and again in 1881 to $35,000 to pay all reservation expenses. The buffalo were gone. Other game animals had been so reduced that their numbers were insufficient. The laws of the United States caused great change in the Blackfoot lifestyle. Polygamy, exchange of women, theft, assault, and the misuse of alcohol were no longer accepted. Murder was punishable by death.

The Indians had their own code. The tribes were left to govern their own conduct. In 1875, tribal law, combined with the law of the land ruled. Law on the reservation was upheld by Indian police. Tribal officers arrested both Indians and whites for their crimes.

Treaties were written by the government and in 1877 the Blackfoot Indians signed and settled onto reservations in southern Alberta. Today, the Blackfoot Crossing Historic Park Interpretive Centre stands on the very location.

In 1882, the Blackfoot held the last buffalo hunt. Later that year, without the buffalo, thousands of hungry Blackfoot Indians amassed around the Badger Creek Agency. They were starving with only government annuities for survival, but there were no rations at the agency. The following harsh winter was known to the Indians as "starvation winter," when hundreds of Piegan died. So many of the Indian people died at the agency they named it, "ghost ridge." Life on the Plains as they had known it was gone forever.

Chippewa Indians, from the east, made war on the Blackfoot. The Piegan last fought the Cree until 1886. Their custom of life on the warpath was ending; it was time for peace.

Land hearings were purposefully held in the bitter cold and only a few of the chiefs attended. The Act of Congress of 1887 was passed. With settlers living all around the reservation, they began making demands for more land. The government negotiated another land treaty. The treaty negotiations were held in sub-zero weather so the Indians would not attend. The agreement was that the reservation be divided into three separate agencies, and the Indians would relinquish all but 45 square miles of land in exchange for $125,000 a year for ten years. A minority of Indians attended. The Blackfoot ceded millions of acres.

The conversion to the reservation was a difficult one and the courageous Blackfoot had already lost half of their populations to the white man's smallpox epidemic. At times, blankets were given to the Indians that were fully infested with a deadly disease. One fourth of their people died because of alcohol-related deaths. The Blackfoot lost many people to Army massacres. Thousands faced starvation due to the massive slaughter of the buffalo. The buffalo literally vanished from the Plains.

In 1888, when the U.S. Government ordered them onto the reservation in northwestern Montana, they offered no resistance and complied. The Army confiscated their horses and shot them in order to contain the Indians there. They lost their valuable buffalo horse, the Spanish Mustang. In 1896, the Blackfoot relinquished their western territory for the sum of $1,500,000. In 1910, it became Glacier National Park. Chief White Calf told of losing their sacred Mount *Ninastako* or Chief Mountain, saying that it was like losing one of his members.

Currently, the tribal headquarters for five reservations are at their agency in Browning, Montana. Reservation towns include Babb, Blackfoot, Glacier Homes, Heart Butte, Kiowa and Seville. Tribal lands are leased for farms, grazing, homes and commercial use. Tribal members have the first choice to lease.

The Blackfeet Nation has an attractive medium blue flag with 29 feathers on a coup stick portrayed there. In the center is a ring of 32 black and white eagle feathers, which surrounds their reservation map. The tribal name appears in Algonquian and in English.

Their populations had rebounded and built back up to 12,000 people by 1950. Today, 25,000 members make up the Blackfoot Nation. 15,000 Blackfoot live in Canada. The Blackfoot tribe in Canada is referred to as a First Nation. There are four tribes of Blackfoot today. Three exist in Canada and one in Montana. Each tribe has its own reservation and land to live on and govern.

The Indian reservation is One Nation; the tribe has its own lands that they can reside on and are able to govern. The passage of the Indian Religious Freedom Act of 1978 gave the Blackfeet Nation the right to practice their age-old religion. Most Blackfoot people speak English. A smaller percentage speaks the Native tongue today. The Blackfoot language is taught in the elementary schools on the reservation at Browning. It is boasted that 50% of the population know Blackfeet and that it is still spoken.

The Great Northern Reservation is the home of 10,000 resident members of the Blackfeet Nation and has an enrollment of 14,000 members. If an Indian is quarter blood Blackfeet, he is eligible to enroll in the tribe. In 1990, there were 38,000 Blackfoot people in America and 11,000 in Canada. A major source of Tribal income is oil and natural gas. In 1982, there were 643 producing oil wells and 47 gas wells.

The Blackfeet Indian Reservation is located in the Rocky Mountains in northwest Montana, east of Glacier National Park on the Canadian border and occupies much of Glacier County. Three mountains on the reservation are Chief, *Ninaki* and Papoose, some with elevations over 9,000 feet. The reservation makes up one and one-half million acres of land.

The terrain on the reserve is mountainous, hilly, grassy and forested with conifer trees.

Water bodies are Birch Creek, Cut Bank River, Milk River and St. Mary River, with eight major lakes.

The Northern Blood Nation (Kainai people) reside in Alberta, Canada. In 1882, a surveyor, J.D. Nelson, found the property for the Blood Reserve to be 708.4 miles, with the southern boundary being within 9 miles of the international border. In 1883, the reserve was reduced to 547.5 square miles. The Blood Tribe never accepted those changes; instead, they accepted the original agreement, according to what was identified by Chief Red Crow in 1880. He had not been consulted on the changes of the reserve between the 1882 and 1883 surveys. The Kainai Reserve is the largest in Canada. The Great Spirit allowed the Indian separate nations. The Blood people maintain an attitude of independence and a fierce pride as the Kainai. The Indian native draws strength from his past with a strong vision for the future.

The Northern Peigan reserve is located along Highway #3 between the town of Pincher Creek and Fort McLeod and includes the town of Brocket, Alberta. It is 200 kilometers south of Calgary, at the junction of Highway #2 and secondary Road #505. The original treaties were signed while the Peigan lived along the Oldman River, west of Lethbridge, in Alberta. Canadian Piegan have treaty rights (dual citizenship) to cross the American-Canadian border anytime and they also have dual citizenship. Their counterparts in America do not.

The Canadian Piegan spell their name (ei), while the Montana Piegan spell their name, (ie). Canadian Blackfoot is spelled with two o's, while Montana Blackfeet use the spelling, ee. Each reserve is an independent nation. They have their own flag. There is a chief and a ruling council of twelve elders. The Piegan seek economic independence and self-determination. They create business ventures and employment. In 1986, a high school was added to the existing elementary schools.

The Northern Siksika Nation is located an hour's drive east of Calgary, Canada, just three kilometers south of Trans Canada Highway # 1. The Administrative Office and business district are strategically located next to the town of Gleichen, to accommodate the visitors. The Siksika have approximately 6,000 members, part of the Blackfeet Confederacy, which includes the Piikuni and Kainaiwa of southern Alberta and the Blackfeet in the state of Montana. The Northern Siksika Nation is governed by a chief and twelve council members. The current chief of the tribe is Stater

156

Crowfoot. The Siksika nation is presently in the process of developing a framework that will provide a self-governing body in order to control the destiny of the Siksika people, free of Canada's Indian Act of 1876.

The Blackfeet Nation is known as a tribe in America and the Blackfoot are referred to as a First Nation in Canada. Each tribe has its reservation. Every reservation is its own entity, like a small country. The Indians make and uphold their own laws and government. They elect governing officials by consensus and have their own flags. There are 25,000 members of the Blackfoot Nation making up four bands 10,000 live in America, while 15,000 dwell in Canada.

Famous Blackfoot chiefs and medicine men were Black Bear, Calf Shirt, Captain Jack, Crop-Eared-Wolf, Crowfoot (*Isapo-muxika*), Eagle's Ribs, Iron Shirt (*Mehkskehme Sukahs*), Heavy Runner, Earl Old Person, Generous Woman, Lame Bull, Little Plume, Mountain Chief, (*Ninastoko*), Old Woman (Ermine Horses), Red Crow, Sitting White Buffalo, Three Suns, Two Guns, White Calf, 13 Yellow Horse, and Medicine Calf.

*****

# CONCLUSION

The Blackfoot Indians originated on the North American continent in a land that would become Alberta, Canada. There is no emperical evidence that they migrated west from the Great Lakes region. Actually, dwelling in Alberta, isolated from the Great Lakes Algonquian speakers, seemed to produce a completely different dialect that appeared to fall off the language stock first. The 6,000 year-old buffalo jump in Alberta, Heads Smashed in Buffalo Jump has had continuous use to historic times, indicating the Blackfoot involvement there.

Their origin in Alberta made up the Blackfoot Confederacy of the Blackfoot, Blood, Piegan, and Small Robes tribes. The southern Piegan pushed southward across the Rocky Mountains and into the land that would become Montana and became Plains Indians and hunters of buffalo. They followed the herds and moved their camps, living as nomads. The Blackfoot Indian used the domestic dog to pull a travois to move his goods.

The Blackfoot tribe had bands, clans and societies. Their societies provided much of the social life. They smoked the pipe, danced, skits, and mock war. Societies were adapted for both men and women.

A head chief or head man was elected by the people to lead. He did their bidding. The head chief was to be a proven warrior. A hunt leader was also a chosen position. The council, under the head chief, was made up of twelve members. They made the decisions for war, the hunt, the camp move and any other important decisions. The council enforced rules and taboos.

The medicine man or shaman was the religious leader of the band. He performed magic and administered healing. The shaman might go into a trance while healing the sick.

It was traditional for the women to do the camp work. They gathered nuts, berries, seeds and grasses, carried wood and water. The women kept the teepees. They tanned hides and made the clothing. Blackfoot women bore the children and cared for them. Occasionally, women went to war.

The Blackfoot had few sociopolitical allies. Their old ally was the Sarcee tribe. In Montana, their allies were the Hidatsa. This tribe became their enemies in the Nineteenth Century and was blamed wrongly for something that they did not do. The arrival of the white man began with Lewis and Clark, other explorers, fur trade companies and free-trappers. French fur trappers came early and inter-married with the Indians, living among them. In the mid-1800's, Jesuit priests arrived among the Blackfoot.

The Plains Indians' whole livelihood depended on the buffalo. Clothing, meat, moccasins, robes, tipi skins, tools, and utensils came from the buffalo. The arrival of the horse totally revolutionized their life way. It gave them mobility to travel, hunt and make war.

Counting coup and taking scalps was a way of warfare that they adopted. The Blackfeet warriors became fierce, warring Indians preying on nearby tribes, taking horses, scalps, slaves and plunder.

The Indian Wars in the northwest began in the 1850's; although war with the Blackfeet Indians and the United States was never declared. The Blackfeet warriors did enough to provoke war. The Blackfeet braves attacked and retreated across the medicine line into Canada safely. Pioneer wagons rolled west into Indian Territory and there was strife between them. The immigrants chose Indian land to graze livestock. Miners clamored over their lands. Fur traders trapped out their streams. The buffalo were shot and left to rot. Settlers wanted their best lands.

Peace treaties with the government were signed with the Indians. that reduced millions of acres of Indian land to small parcels where the Indians could live on reservations. A government act called for the buffalo to be shot; the bison nearly died off. The fighting stopped. Indians went onto reservations. The Army shot their horses to limit their movement. The white man introduced measles and smallpox; half their numbers died off.

When the buffalo became scarce in the late 1800's, the Piegan were encouraged to convert to agriculture. They were reduced to farmers and many starved. Finally, some took up ranching and farming, and many liked it. They did not like it much and instead, turned to ranching. There are numerous successful Blackfeet Indian ranchers on the reservation today.

The Spanish Mustang and buffalo have been reintroduced to the reserve. Reservations today produce work for the Blackfeet people. There are schools and churches. American Indians are successful college graduates.

In 1925, Robert Brislawn, an Oshto, Wyoming rancher, decided to try and save the Spanish Mustang for the Blackfoot Indians. He bought all of the Mustangs that he could find and began to breed them. In 1957, the Spanish Mustang Registry was founded. Mustangs with the right blood lines were registered. Jack Hines, a western artist, visited the ranch and saw his mustangs. He later met Bob Black Bull on the Blackfeet reservation in northern Montana. Hines gave him two mustangs that he had bought from the Brislawn ranch. Black Bull sold Hines several pieces of artwork. He used the money to buy six mustang mares.

These horses made up the first herd of buffalo horses in Blackfoot hands since the 1800's. Word of the buffalo runners spread and a large crowd of Indians greeted Black Bull and his horses. The Army had all but obliterated the Spanish Mustang. Black Bull called the horses a lifeline to the past. In 1994, the Blackfeet Buffalo Horse Coalition was founded. Black Bull established a leasing program and a colt exchange for the preservation of the Blackfoot buffalo runners. In addition, the Blackfeet Indian tribe now has a National Buffalo Reserve on the reservation.

In 1980, the Blackfeet Community College was established in Browning, Montana. The college offers Intermediate Blackfeet language classes along with a history of their people.

Native traditions have not been forgotten. Annual powwows and dances are held throughout the year. Their annual North American Indian Days is held on the reservation at the powwow grounds, near the Plains Indian Museum in Browning. There is a powwow, festivities, socializing and museum tours. Powwows include powwow dances, drummers, music, songs and storytelling. Indians in traditional dress perform. Tourists come by the thousands to attend.

### Winold Reiss

Winold Reiss was a German immigrant, who immigrated to America in 1913. Born in the Black Forest of Germany, Winold learned to paint from his father, Fritz Reiss, a well-known painter of the time. He followed in his father's footsteps and became a master painter. Inspired by the novels of James Fennimore Cooper, Winold pursued his dream of knowing more about the Native American Indians.

His oil paintings centered on the American Indians, and many of Mr. Reiss's portraits were painted on the Blackfoot Indian Reservation in Browning, Montana. Reiss has recorded an era in American Indian history. Winold Reiss pioneered the decorative art form in America and painted hundreds of paintings of the Blackfoot Indians.

In 1943, in just ninety days, the brilliant artist painted 75 portraits of them. The Blackfoot Indians inducted Winold into their tribe on August 29, 1943, and gave him the name, "Beaver Child." He was truly a gifted man and a highly talented artist. Beaver Child went to rest on August 29, 1953 and his ashes were scattered over the very Blackfoot land that he loved. He was 92. Currently, Winold Reiss's paintings are on display at the Denver Art Museum. The wonderful painting career of Winold Reiss with the Blackfoot has become his legacy.

160

#46. "Nobody has Pity on Me,"
Like most Blackfeet youths, is proficient at hunting, fishing and sports.
He is an excellent student, an active member of the Future Farmers of
America.

Print Courtesy of BNSF Railway

#47. "Short Man/Piegan"
Short Man, master of the Pecunnie Indian sign language, and highly
respected member of the tribe, also known among his people as Big Left
Arm.  He lived until his eighty sixth year.

Print Courtesy of Renate Reiss

#48. "Yellow Head, Piegan"
Yellow Head is one of the handsomest men of the Pecunnies. Educated in government school, he speaks fluent English, but still adheres to the traditions of his forefathers.

Print Courtesy of Renate Reiss

163

#49. "Many Guns, Full Blood Blackfeet"
Tom Many Guns is a full blooded Blackfeet Indian rancher living on the
Blackfeet Indian Reservation in Montana. He has been helpful to the
film industry, and has recorded more than a hundred native songs.

Print Courtesy of Renate Reiss

#50. "Striped Wolf, Blood Tribesman"
Striped Wolf, a prominent member of the Bloods, and recognized by his
People as a man of excellent judgment. His record as a great hunter and
Warrior earned him the lasting gratitude and respect of his people.

Print Courtesy of Renate Reiss

#51. "Mike Oka"
Mike Oka was present as a boy at the signing of the Treaty of Blackfeet Crossing in 1877 between the Canadian government and the Indians. For years he served as Indian scout with the Royal Northwest Mounted.

Print Courtesy of Renate Reiss

#52. "Dancing Boy, Blackfeet"
Dancing Boy's family name is Calvin Last Star. He is recognized as one of
the most accomplished dancers among the Blackfeet. Thousands of visitors
to Glacier National Park enjoy his fine dancing ability.
Print Courtesy of Renate Reiss

#53. "The Drummers"
Sure Chief, Buffalo Body and Heavy Breast…make a drummer combo hard to beat.
The Blackfeet are a musical people who love to drum and sing on all occasions.
Print Courtesy of Renate Reiss

#54. "Many Mules"
Many Mules, a venerable old warrior of the Blood Tribe, was eighty-two
years old, almost blind and rode thirty-two miles on horseback to have this
portrait of himself painted.
Print Courtesy of Renate Reiss

#55. "Crow Chief, Blackfeet"
Born in 1876, Crow Chief has been an outstanding leader in reservation politics who has earned the respect and esteem of his people. His service on the Tribal Council spans half a century.
Print Courtesy of Renate Reiss

# Index

## Bibliography

Aikens, Melvin C., Anthropological Papers, # 93, Hogup Cave, University of Utah, Salt Lake, 1979.

Bains, Rae, Indians of the Plains, Troll Associates, Mahwah, New Jersey, 1985.

Brown, Dee, The Story of the Plains Indians, National Historic Society, Gettysburg, 1973.

Capps, Benjamin, The Great Chiefs, Time Life Books, Alexandria,1975.

Convis, Charles L., Mountain Men, Pioneer Press, Carson City, 1997.

Convis, Charles L., Native American Women, Pioneer Press, Carson City, 1996.

Convis, Charles L., Warriors & Chiefs of the Old West, Pioneer Press, Carson City, 1996.

Dunn, J.P., Massacres of the Mountains, Archer House, Inc., New York, 1886.

Ewers, John C., The Blackfeet, Raiders on the Northwestern Plains, University of Oklahoma Press, Norman, 1958.

Grant, Bruce, Concise Encyclopedia of American Indians, Random House, New York, 1989.

Grinell, George Bird, Blackfoot Indian Stories, Riverbend Publishing, Helena, 2005.

Grinell, George Bird, Blackfoot Lodge Tales, A Bison Book, Lincoln, 1962.

Hungry Wolf, Adolph & Beverly, Indian Tribes of the Northern Rockies, Good Medicine Books, 1989.

Liptak, Karen, North American Indian Sign Language, Franklin Watts, New York, 1990.

Lowie, Robert H., Indians of the Plains, McGraw-Hill Book Company, New York, 1954.

Mails, Thomas E., The Mystic Warriors of the Plains, New York, Doubleday Publishing Company, 1972.

McClintock, Walter, The Old North Trail, Bison Books, Lincoln, Nebraska, 1999.

Schaefer, Dr. Claude E., The Story of the Blackfoot Indians, Great Northern Railway, St. Paul, 1858.

Shultz, James Willard, Blackfeet and Buffalo, University of Oklahoma Press, Norman, 1962.

Steber, Rick, Mountain Men, Bonanza Publishing Company, Prineville, Oregon, 1990.

Terrell, John Upton, American Indian Almanac, Barnes and Noble, New York, 1971.

Walker, Wyman D., The Wild Horse of the West, Caxton Printers, Ltd., Caldwell, Idaho, 1945.

Whistler, Clark, Indians of the United States, Doubleday & Company, Inc., Garden City, New York, 1966.

Zimmerman, Larry J., Native North America, Duncan-Baird Publishers, London, 1996.

## Citing Electronic Publications

<http: //www.aaanativearts.com/article1409.html>

<http://www.accessgeneology.com/native/tribes/blackfeet/war.htm>

<http: //www.answers.com/topic/algonquian-algonquin-algonquian- language>

<http: //www.answers.com/topic/Washakie>

<http://www.big orrin.org/blackfoot_kids.htm>

<http://www.blackfeet.aaanativearts.com/>

<http: //www.//en.wikipedia.org/wiki/Louisiana_Purchase>

<http: //www.//en.wikipedia.org/wiki/Algonquian_languages>

<http: //www.head-smashed-in.com/frmblack.html>

<http:/ /www.idahohistory.net/Reference%20Series/0286.pdf>

<http://www.museumtrail.org/OldSpanishTrail.asp>

<http: //www.native-languages.org/blackfoot.htm>

<http://www.native-languages.org/blackfoot-legends.htm>

<http://www.nativepeoples.com/article/articles/121/1/The-Pueblo-Revolt-of-1680/Page1.html>

<http://www.pc.gc.ca/eng/lhn-nhs/ob/rocky/mountain/index-aspx>

<http://www.snowowl.com/peopleblackfoot.html>

<http://www.trail tribes.org/greatfalls/shrinking-reservation.htm>

<http://www.Trail tribes.org/lemhi/whos-who.htm>

<http://www.answers.com/topic/washakie>

## Glossary

Aborigine-A native inhabitant or the earliest people to live in a region.
Archeology-the scientific study of material remains of past human life and activities.
Arrowhead-a triangular shaped arrow tip, chipped from stone to penetrate an animal.
Arrow- a slender featheredshaft shot from a bow used to hunt or in battle.

175

Artifact-early tool used by the ancient peoples.

Awl-pointed stone hand tool for making holes in leather for clothing.

Band- is an extended family group or conjoined group of peoples.

Bone whistle-a small musical instrument made of eagle bone.

Bow-a flexible strip of wood, bent by sinew between its ends, used to shoot an arrow.

Coup-is the art of touching the enemy Indian with a quirt or stick, either on foot or horseback.

Culture-artistic and intellectual pursuit and products of the Plains Indians.

Drill cup-a hand stone with a partially drilled hole used to retain the shaft of a bow-drill.

Encampment-temporary campsite used by aborigines.

Extended family- is a large nuclear family.

Fauna-Animal life that is specific to a certain time period or special environment.

Flora-is plants that are specific to or characteristic of a region.

Fort-A fortified stronghold occupied by troops, settlers or fur trappers.

Garb-the kind of clothing worn by the Indians.

Great Divide- The watershed of North America formed by the Rocky Mountains separating streams flowing west from flowing east.

Haft-to attach a handle to a tool or an arrowhead to a shaft.

Head man-The lesser chief of a primitive community.

Lithic-made from stone as a tool or arrowhead.

Peck-method of removing small pieces from a stone in shaping a tool.

Pithouse-a prehistoric Indian dwelling dug below ground using saplings covered with earth with a tunneled entrance at one end.

Scalp lock-A long tuft of otherwise shaved head, especially of a warrior of some tribes.

Sororate polygyny-was the practice of a man marrying his bride's younger sisters.

Squaw is non-offensive Narraganset Indian word for girl, woman or wife.

War bonnet -is a ceremonial headdress, often with a feather extension down the back.

## Author explores inside of a 19th century stone house in southeastern Oregon. About the Author

Born in Lexington, Nebraska, Robert Bolen, B.A. has a degree in Archeology/Anthropology. In an Archeology class, he was informed that because of his features, the Mongolian Eye-fold, he was part Indian. In 1755, a Bolen ancestor was taken captive by Delaware Indians. She was later rescued with her baby daughter, Robb's Great, Great, Grandmother. At the time of rescue, the poor girl (just 17) was scalped, but she lived. The French scalp was the size of a silver dollar. Family says that she combed her hair hiding the scar and managed to live to be well over one hundred years of age. Bolen's served under George Washington in the American Revolution. In 1777, the author's ancestors erected Fort Bolin, near Cross Creek, Pennsylvania for protection from Indian attacks. Two ancestors were killed in Kentucky by Shawnee Indians allied to the British. Great Gran-dad Gilbert Bolen rode with the Ohio Fourth Cavalry in the Civil War under General Sherman. In 1866, Gilbert brought his wife and six children west to Nebraska in a Conestoga wagon. Gran-dad Denver Colorado Bolen knew Buffalo Bill Cody in western Nebraska. Bolen is an authority on Indian artifacts and glass trade beads. Robb and Dori Bolen reside in Nampa, Idaho, near Boise. Robb owns the website, Fort Boise Bead Trader.com.

# PHOTOGRAPHS

# COURTESY OF

# AZUSA Publishing, LLC

# 3575 S. Fox Street

# Englewood, CO 80110

**Email: azusa@azusapublishing.com**

**Phone Toll-free: 888-783-0077**

**Phone/Fax: 303-783-0073**

**Email:** azusa@azusapublishing.com

Mailing address: P.O. Box 2526, Englewood, CO 80150

JERRY LEE YOUNG'S
IDAHO HERITAGE MUSEUM
2390 HWY. 93 SOUTH #B
TWIN FALLS, IDAHO 83301

CPSIA information can be obtained
at www.ICGtesting.com
Printed in the USA
FFOW05n0010050814

9 781599 759999